COSTUMES AND SETTINGS FOR HISTORICAL PLAYS

Volume 3
The Elizabethan
and Restoration Period

COSTUMES AND SETTINGS FOR HISTORICAL PLAYS

JACK CASSIN-SCOTT

Volume 3
The Elizabethan
and Restoration Period

B T Batsford Limited London

First published 1979
ISBN 0 7134 1706 4

Printed in Great Britain by
The Anchor Press Limited
Tiptree Essex
for the publishers
B T Batsford Limited
4 Fitzhardinge Street
London W1H 0AH

CONTENTS

INTRODUCTION

This third volume in the Costumes and Settings for Historical Plays Series covers the interesting period of almost two centuries of fashion from 1550 to 1715.

The art of costume is nowhere more apparent than in the world of the theatre and entertainment. Here they can be seen and used to convey to an audience all the psychological importance of characterisation. The designer has the means, through costume, to tell the audience, without the spoken word, all there is to know about the character, his/her occupation, social standing and other important facets. The costume must have an immediate impact on the entrance of the actor and quickly establish his role in the plot, as time is the essence in any play. The designer must therefore work in close relationship both with the producer and actor, to interpret and bring to life — in fact larger than life size — the character portrayed in the script, through costume.

It must be emphasised again and again to the would-be designer of this period that carefully planned exaggeration is an essential factor in theatrical costume. Every unusual facet must be seized upon and slightly stressed, colours increased in bold brilliant arrangements almost to the point of crudeness, if it heightens the impact of the play. The study of all elements for essential research on costume should come to the attention of the designer. A beautiful and well executed costume can fade to insignificance if too much attention, for example, has been paid to elaborate fine detail, and not, to the overall silhouette and colour. Shapes in silhouette and colour are all important to stage representation. Authenticity is highly desirable and recommended, but not at the expense of the production as a whole. Accentuated headdresses, waistlines, frills and colour combinations add a panache to the play.

Each epoch had its fashionable costume silhouette which was sufficient unto itself, and the designer must create this

The lady on the right with a high closed sleeveless winged bodice with a slashed front. The sleeves of the undergarment were straight with small ruff cuffs. The high neck was sur- mounted with a small ruff. Long false hanging sleeves were present. The open skirt revealed the petticoat. A small close to the head hat was worn. The lady on the right is wearing the open robe with close fitting bodice and short puffed sleeves and long undergarment sleeves. The overskirt opening reveals the petticoat. A close fitting coif was worn with a flat hat   c 1590

7

to allow the era to exist for the moment of the play.

Architecture is as important as costume: both represent the differences between classes of society. In this period, as in others, there must exist a close relationship between the style of setting and the style of costume. The sixteenth century horizontal forms found expression in the architecture of antique inspiration. The Spanish and French farthingales, the bombasted shoulders and deep collars gave squareness to women's silhouettes which followed the male style of broad shoulders and shoe designs, and the characteristic design of the doublets which followed. The Elizabethan plays showed in vivid action an age of violent contrasts.

The period of the middle sixteenth century, from which this volume begins, reflects the heavy, artificial splendour of the Spanish fashion which remained in vogue for three-quarters of a century. The functional purpose of the costume seemed of little importance, what mattered most was the effect — the decorative effect which was surely a designer's dream. The stiff dark material which was the fashionable image of the period became a background for the encrusted jewels with which many of the dresses were adorned, was also a sign of wealth.

The human frame inside these costumes was subjected to a confusion of torturous aids, nothing was natural or simple; shoulders, waists, stomachs and hips were constricted, corseted, padded, wired, bejewelled and distorted, moulded into man's fashionable style. The hair was shaven, fluffed, curled, bejewelled or dyed (in various hues). Faces were painted and patched.

The influence of Spain was more than a mere whim of fashion, it was steeped in politics. The powerful position of the Spanish Empire under Charles V, who ruled over Germany, Austria, Netherlands and vast possessions both in America and Africa, made the Spanish presence felt, and Spanish fashion had to be accepted in the subjugated countries.

The development of the newly found lands of the Americas should not be underestimated. It became apparent in the flow and profusion of exotic styles in the precious metal and jewelled decoration. Within this age of discovery, fashionable costume of men and women closely resembled each other, both in design and richness of decorative and elaborately woven patterns. Each era produced a distinctive style, although the tailorship remained fairly constant.

The lady is wearing the French high waisted soft falling full skirt with a square décolletage with full sleeves finishing with a small turned back lace cuff. The man is wearing a doublet with puffed out sleeves paned from the shoulders then straight to the wrist ending in a small ruff. He is wearing gathered trunk hose and short canions, and high soft leather boots. Round the neck he has a falling ruff. Around him is draped a short full cloak. He wears a large hat with feathers   c 1625

Details of accessories for the wealthier classes, which reflected more the personal taste of the period, came and went according to artistic and social demands, yet working people's clothes reflected more the different conditions of reality rather than artistic fancies. It is essential to remember in so far as 'creation' is concerned.

In this volume I have attempted to offer some practical advice to the set designer whose job it is to give a sense of illusion and atmosphere to the production. It is important to realise from the outset that he or she must combine craftsmanship along with a visionary idea, never letting one outstrip the other, and basing both on the practical limitations of the stage available. The open air theatres of the Elizabethan era and the architectural multiple setting system of the Italian School played a great part in the scenic design of the European theatre producing spectacular effects. There are many good books written by experts on these periods of the theatre, read them carefully, much of what is achieved today comes from the experiments of design and materials to create the scenic effects now used.

The illustrations follow the lines of the previous books in this series, clear and simplified drawings taken wherever possible from contemporary sources.

Stage properties cover the weapons and armour of the soldiers. But under the same heading come furniture, jewellery, musical instruments and domestic utensils.

Stage lighting is discussed in brief detail because light and colour have a definite place in the set. Its greatest function is to emphasise the mood of the play, that is, to create atmosphere.

Briefly I want to open the doors of the workshops that you may look in and see the theatre at work.

THE COSTUME

Designing and creating stage costumes begins with a play reading. From there the designer starts to apply his/her knowledge and know-how.

First consideration is the period of the play, then comes the mammoth job of essential research. This is a designer's greatest problem if it is not carried out in a firm diligent manner, many will be the pitfalls. Research the facts correctly and the production, costume-wise, will be that more professional. A careful study of detail will result in a costume worthy of the play. Each production is a challenge, and each costume an individual creation. So to begin, bear these facts in mind: first study the play and the period, secondly study carefully the character to be costumed and thirdly never leave out obvious detail.

For the would-be designer there are many books on the subject of fashion, so consult them. Museums, some with good collections of clothes of all periods, visit them. Art galleries, with many fine contemporary pictures, are well worth a visit. All these are there to be perused and used. They are in fact the costume-designer's 'tools of the trade' and their slogan must always be 'research and more research'.

Before a production meeting it is well worth a little forward investigation to form an impression of the characters to be dressed. A rough sketch of the basic costume is sufficient, at this stage, as it is unlikely that the person who will eventually play the role will have already been chosen. If however the designer has some pre-knowledge, so much the better as it is always helpful to base the costume on the actual person. But more often than not, the designer can never dress the person of his own choosing, so my advice is to wait and see — the eventual creation of a costumed character is always the interesting challenge of stage costume designing.

So, armed with the rough basic outline of the costume,

Middle class women wearing the high closed bodice and neck ruff. On the left the lady has puffed full short sleeves with straight undergarment sleeves. The open overskirt reveals the petticoat. She wore a tall rounded hat with a narrow brim and feather decoration. The lady on the right has a short shoulder cape with a turned down collar. An apron covers the overskirt opening and the petticoat. She is wearing a small crowned hat and slouched brim and a chin clout c 1590

the first conference can be faced with confidence and will certainly help to get an early response to the ultimate idea of how the character should be dressed. In designing, remember quite clearly the epoch and its fashionable silhouette and you will not go wrong. Also it is important to note that a costume was not worn merely because it was necessary, but because it represented, by means of its form, the period of the time, the social status and above all the character of the individual.

The study of all the elements concerning materials should come to the attention of the designer of stage costume. The study of dye, for example, can show the period of its use and give the time and place of its wearing. It must also be remembered that this particular period was an era of voluntary emigration caused by economical and political upheaval. In 1567 England allowed the influx of Flemish weavers to settle and they brought with them their manufacturing processes. This, coupled with the wool trade, established further new designs and fabrics. The maritime discoveries of The New World brought about the extraordinary fashions of the second half of the sixteenth century. The new woven patterns and new ornamentation produced extreme artificial, ugly elegance. Padding was the outrageous fashion, making both male and female figures into exaggerated and monstrous shapes.

For men the trunk hose was the characteristic garment of the *Elizabethan period*, giving a pumpkin-shaped hipline. The hose was frequently divided into vertical 'panes' with contrasting lining colour being visible in the space between. This is an essential silhouette in any revival of Elizabethan plays which were popular between 1550-1600. From 1570 these were often worn with canions, short breeches underneath extending to the knees. The doublet was usually padded, stiff, wasp-waisted and tight, this must be made to give a very smooth appearance. Sometimes they were 'pinked or slashed' revealing a contrasting coloured lining. Possible modern materials for making this costume and others mentioned in this chapter would be unbleached calico, wool jersey, cambric, velveteen and sateen. Under stage lighting conditions these give excellent results when dyed, stencilled or sprayed.

Such is the stage costume designer's lot that, having lost the fundamental art of a costume creation which once existed, he or she has to re-create it, using modern methods and materials whilst still retaining the original silhouette.

Such a garment is the farthingale, sometimes in large dimensions, shaped by graduated hoops becoming wider towards the hem, making a bell-shape, or with regular hoops giving a drum shape, both covering the lower limbs, giving the women a gliding movement. Above the waist the bodice followed the male doublet style which flattened the breasts.

Hats were worn by men and women inside and outside the home, these add a further course of study for the costume designer as they were a most fashionable necessity, velveteen and felt being the best possible materials to be used.

The gradual change of costume came in about the second decade of the seventeenth century. Elizabethan fashions were replaced by the less rigid fashion of the cavalier modes. Lace being worn in abundance, as was seen by the ruffs which were the hall-mark of the period. These, when well made, add great charm and authenticity to the costume. Cloaks also became fashionable being slung diagonally around the body or hung over one shoulder. These came in various lengths and the young designer can make full play of this particular garment, especially with any flamboyant character within the production.

Low crowned hats with wide brims bedecked with sweeping plumes add gaiety and style to the costume of the period. The high waist lines affected allow full swinging movement to the long pleating of the skirts and breeches. Massed gathered-up drapery gives bold deep folds which, when catching the light, give a richness and liveliness to the material and, with the further application of feathers and ribbons what further scope can the costume designer ask for.

The *Baroque period* of fashion displayed the beautiful materials with heavy drapery intermingled with satins, velvets and fine feathers.

The violent years between 1620-1660 with wars and rebellion throughout Europe brought sombre clothes. *The Commonwealth period* in England turns the costume designers mind to materials of blacks, browns and greys, with a noticeable absence of lace, along with jerkins and buff leather jackets, of steel lobster-pot helmets, of heavy military jack-boots and heavy swords.

The petticoat-breeches fashion (Rhinegraves) resembled a divided skirt, but here again the designer has a rare subject on which to embellish, with the short bolero-type waistcoats, full breeches adorned with bunches of ribbons, and

A close fitting bodice with large puffed sleeves and straight sleeves of the undergarment showing. The skirt was full over which was an apron. The neck was encircled with a ruff and on the head was a close fitting coif over the ears and the forehead   c 1590

tall, stiff crowned hats with wide brims, also frequently edged with decorative bunches of ribbon.

The *Restoration period*, or the age of formality, brought with it the most sudden and abrupt revolutionary emergence of changes in the male attire, which set a standard for all the fashionable men throughout England and Europe. By 1670 this new fashion was firmly established and was the accepted costume for almost the whole of the coming century.

The long coat with flared skirts which were long to the knee, was buttoned down the front which generally remained unbuttoned revealing a long waistcoat and was, in all respects, a similar garment to the coat; neither had revers. The falling band collar lost favour and was replaced with a cravat. The loose baggy Rhinegraves also passed out of fashion and breeches of a closer fit were worn. But the most extraordinary fashion was the wig. Although wigs had been worn on and off for the last few thousand years, it was in this period that they reached their zenith. For the costume designer of this period it is important that a good knowledge of the art of wigs and wigmaking is essential. The styles were numerous and the variety of wigs increased with each fad of fashion.

The interesting introduction to the fashion for the female in the 1690s was the fontange or tower headdress, also known in England as the 'top knot'. It was a structure of stiff linen or lace frills built tier over tier to a considerable height, and makes an interesting item for costume design.

The many accessories must not be forgotten, from the face make-up of patches to the use of muffs and walking canes, all of which make a stage costume design come to life.

Elizabethan (Spanish fashion) 1558-1603

The marriage of Philip II, son of Charles V who succeeded his father in Spain, Burgundy and the Netherlands, to Mary Tudor Queen of England, brought about an increase of the Spanish influence in dress in England.

The progressive and reformatory movements which had started in the early Renaissance period were now being

Goneril

Lady in the formal overgarment hitched up to reveal the dress beneath with the neck surmounted by a small ruff. She is wearing the popular French hood   c 1554

ruthlessly destroyed in the countries over which the mighty Hapsburgs reigned. The difference between the dress of the ordinary people and that of the court which earlier had diminished, was now reaching an impossible gulf. The fashionable image of the period was the dark coloured uncomfortable costume with the high stiff, starched collar. The introduction of starch in 1564 caused the ruffs to become even larger and stiffer, reaching ridiculous proportions and aptly called 'millstones'.

The Englishman, William Lee, invented the first knitting machine for stockings in 1589. He was established in Rouen in France and patronized by Henri IV.

There were at this time many regulations relating to dress. For example, it was not permitted to wear the colour crimson, unless you were of royal blood, and the middle classes were allowed the use of velvet for sleeves only. The baldrick, or shoulder sash of satin, was the fashionable wear for both male and female, but a white sash was worn only by the King. The wearing of coloured fur was restricted to the upper classes. Black was permitted for the lower order. In this period England began to import the Spanish and Italian lace, and both men and women started to adorn their clothes with this costly material. Also introduced into England at about this time was the perfumed leather, in the form of the short Spanish cape and gloves. Although worn in several European countries for some time, and at the court of Henry VIII, it only became fashionable towards the end of the sixteenth century. The perfumed gloves made of satin and velvet fringed with gold, silver or silk were worn by men and women at court. These were known as 'Frangipani gloves'.

Spanish style farthingale. The deep pointed bodice with winged shoulders and long sham sleeves revealing the sleeves of the undergarment with laced cuffs matching the high standing neck ruff c 1570

To a lesser extent the country people followed the Spanish fashion, or as much as they were allowed to adopt. Whilst the legs of the peasant and poor women were covered, a low décolletage was sometimes worn, but on the whole the dress of the ordinary people was both lighter in colour and considerably simpler than the dress of the nobility. White collar and cuffs were worn, but were without the lace trimmings.

Children still wore at this period smaller versions of their elders' clothes.

The decline of the Spanish fashion came as the European countries began to lift the Spanish yoke from themselves. France being the first country to lighten the stiff, unbending dignity of the Spanish costume and introducing a variance of colour and style, with a great deal of extravagance, breaking away completely from the old styles of farthingales, the padding, the stiff starched ruffles and the tight wrists. France remained alone in her new-found freedom of dress for several years. The Spanish style generally throughout Europe continued to be worn, the heavy materials and encrusted ornaments that had decorated the gown and suits in the sixteenth century seemed too expensive both in jewels and material to be cast off so quickly.

Women wore the corseted *bodice*, which was extremely rigid and stiffened with wooden or whalebone stays. The waist was low and deeply pointed in front, and up to about the 1580s was often scallop edged. The bodice was probably

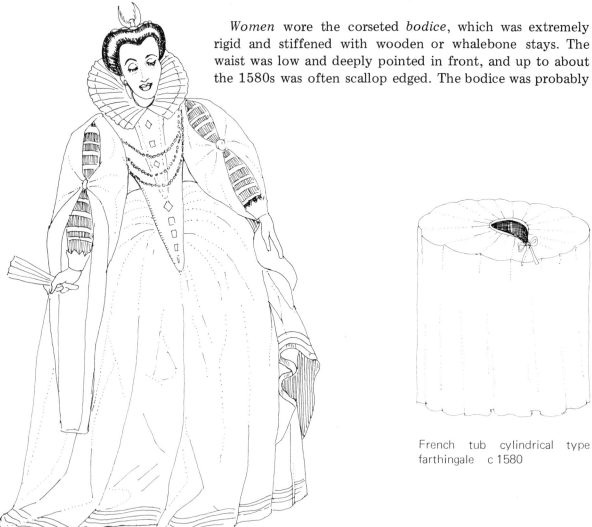

Woman in French farthingale. The long waisted bodice came to a deep centre point over the full skirt. The lace cuffed undergarment sleeves were revealed from under the large hanging sleeves. Hair was drawn off the face   c 1580

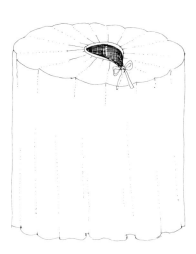

French tub cylindrical type farthingale   c 1580

Bum roll farthingale worn at hip level   c 1575

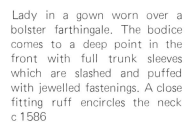

Lady in a gown worn over a bolster farthingale. The bodice comes to a deep point in the front with full trunk sleeves which are slashed and puffed with jewelled fastenings. A close fitting ruff encircles the neck c 1586

fastened down the left side by hooks. The neck-line was low or high; if low it was square cut and arched slightly over the bosom. The low décolletage was covered either by a high necked chemise with a standing collar with a small open frill at the throat, or just with jewellery. The high neck-line had also a standing collar with a small Medici collar. After about 1580 a closed cartwheel type ruff was usually worn. The cuffs at the wrist and other decorations matched the collar, these being either hand ruffs or turn-back cuffs, made in the same material as the neck ruff such as lawn, cambric or lace.

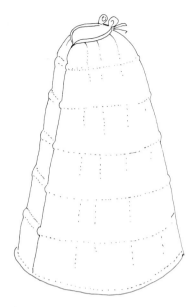

Spanish dome style farthingale
c 1550

Sleeves were close-fitting to the wrist, slightly padded, puffed and slashed finishing with either the hand ruff or turn-back cuffs. The variation of sleeves were with slashed roll wings either double or single or even a large plain roll, or with hanging sleeves, which, after mid-century were often sham. They often matched the dress. There was the close-fitting 'gathered' sleeve, being drawn in by many bands up the arm. The 'bishop' sleeve which was full from the shoulder to the wrist ending with a tight cuff.

Farthingales The long skirts of the wealthy class ladies were usually encrusted with precious metal and stones and sometimes worn open to reveal the rich undergown or petticoat of the same length beneath. This was of a conical shape being supported by a similar shaped undergown of some stiffened material: the forerunner of the crinoline. The Spanish farthingale was in vogue from about 1545-1590, it was also known as a verdigale. It was an under-gown spreading out straight from the waist with circular hoops of wood, steel or whalebone. The shape varied from being a funnel, a bell-shaped or a dome skirt. It was made from canvas, buckram or heavy linen. The overskirt was made to stand stiffly outwards from the waist to the ground, making a smooth surface without any draperies or folds.

The French farthingale became the court fashion in about 1580 and lasted well into the 1620s. There were two styles; the Roll farthingale, known affectionately as the bum roll, which was a padded bolster roll which was worn round the hips, tilted slightly up at the back and tied with tapes in the front. The Wheel farthingale, or Catherine Wheel farthingale, was sometimes called the Italian farthingale, this, as its name implies, was a wheel-shaped structure made from steel or whalebone, usually covered in a damask material. Worn round the waist it had a tilt forward, raised up behind and down at the front, resembling, by the turn of the century as the tilt increased, a large bustle. The skirt was made full enough to be carried out at right angles falling over the farthingale then falling vertically to the feet.

The popular *gown* which was worn for formal occasions and for warmth, was put over the bodice and skirt. The loose-bodied style which had fitted shoulders and fell in folds giving an inverted V shape, opening down the front to reveal the dress beneath; it had a standing collar, open at the throat, fitted sometimes with ties which closed the gown

Close fitting coif and ruff
c 1580

from neck to hem. The sleeves were short and puffed out, with a kick-up effect at the shoulder, they ended just above the elbow. Fitchets which were vertical placket holes often decorated the gown, these served the purpose of enabling articles suspended on the girdle of the skirt to be reached. Popular among the maiden ladies was the Catherine de Medici style of the very low décolletage, which bared the bosom. It is said that Elizabeth of England wore this style in her later years.

The lady is in a close bodied gown with a high standing collar. The bodice had large puffed kick-up sleeves from which emerged the close under-sleeve. The open overskirt reveals the petticoat. She is wearing a version of the Stuart type hood. The boy is in a close fitting doublet and a high standing collar with the skirt and wings a similar design. It was buttoned down the front with a slight peascod. Round the waist was a narrow ribbon belt. He had short full trunk hose   c 1574

21

Rogan

The lady is in a wide flared jacket with large puffed kick-up shoulder sleeves from which emerged the straight sleeves of the undergarment. The stiff and heavy overskirt formed an inverted V shape which revealed the petticoat. A small hat was worn over a jewelled caul. The man is wearing a bombasted jacket, close fitting with a high neck and high waist, with short skirts over a padded pluderhosen and he wore a low crowned barret hat decorated with feathers. He had a short cloak with a collar c 1577

Headwear Feminine *hats* followed the men's style, with brims and feathers, but were generally smaller and worn fairly straight on the head, usually worn over a linen cap. A popular style of bonnet was the Mary Stuart hood made of lawn, cambric or linen, trimmed with lace, its particular feature being the dip to form a curve over the centre of the forehead. Bonnets such as the French hood or bongrace, the cornet, the Taffeta Pipkin and the Lettice Cap were worn. Hats for riding and travelling became popular towards the end of the century, these were of various shapes and materials from felt to beaver.

Wired lace ruff   c 1558

Lady in open gown with deep pointed bodice. The overskirt open from waist to hem reveals the underskirt. The long winged sham sleeves reveal the puffed and slashed sleeves of the undergarment. The neck is encircled with a wide lawn ruff   c 1589

Stuart hood   c 1561

Other *headwear* during this period was in the way of simple head coverings resembling hair nets known as reticulated cauls, covering the back of the head, made from silk or hair. The forehead cloth was a triangular piece of material, with the point at the back, the straight edge round the forehead and tied under the chin, these were worn with coifs, cauls and neckerchiefs. Resembling a large calash was the Arched Hood, made from a thick material, wired along one border, which was bent into a curve to create an arch shape over the head but projected forward over the forehead. The wire supports were either fixed to the shoulders or sometimes as low as the waist. The drapery could be gathered at the back of the neck or the waist, or allowed to hang freely in various lengths down the back. It was not considered correct for ladies to walk bare-headed, or with just head ornamentation. Throughout the period the women wore long hair plaited or coiled behind the head, usually hidden by the headdress, the front hair was always worn away from the forehead but in various styles. If a centre parting was used the hair was waved and bunched out at the sides or turned back over pads giving the fullness at the temples. Without a parting the hair was pulled over a 'palisadoe' or wire frame, which dipped in the centre like a 'widow's peak' widening at the sides.

Hair   False hair, ornamented dressed wigs, feathers and dyed hair were in vogue. The colours red and blond in the dyed hair range being most popular as Elizabeth of England set the fashion of the English court, red dyed hair was a compliment to her.

Beauty aids Powder and rouge were used, and patches made of silk or velvet made into various shapes and sizes were applied to the face by means of mastic.

Footwear   Stockings at this period were either tailor made, or knitted. Silk stockings were worn by the rich and it is stated that Queen Elizabeth was the first Englishwoman to wear them. Embroidered garters were also worn, tied just below the knee, it was in this era that the low-cut shoe with a high heel first appeared and 'pumps' became very popular. The shoes had cork soles with both leather and embroidered velvet for the uppers; worn over the shoes when outdoors was a variety of overshoes and pantofles. Chopines, clogs or pattens, 10 to 18 cm (4 to 7 in.) in height, the pattens ⅃ wooden or cork soles, and the pantofles had cork soles but with the front uppers only.

Accessories   for the costume varied from country to country but mainly consisted of gloves, handkerchiefs, ruffs, bags and fans. Hanging from the girdle was a pomander or dry scent box. Feather fans were carried and black velvet masks were worn in the street. This latter accessory was supposed to protect the face from the elements, leaving the complexion unmarred. Scarves and mufflers were worn, the former for show, made from silk and tasselled in gold or silver, the latter for warmth made from taffeta or velvet. Small muffs were carried, being small and tubular, made in fur and silk, usually they were slung from the girdle.

For men the Spanish influence was now evolving into a definite style. The *doublet* was close-fitting with a short skirt, tight waisted and pointed in front. The 'peascod body' which followed the Dutch fashion was an excessively padded long-pointed projecting front, which overhung the girdle. In England this fashion was less extreme. The doublet was fitted with a standing collar often edged with stiffened tabs, standing out at right angles. The tabs or pickadils were used to support the earlier small ruffs. In the 1570s the collar became high at the back and low in the front to accommodate the larger ruffs. The fastenings of the doublet ran from the collar to the waist by a series of buttons and loops. The doublet body was stiffened with buckram and well padded with wool, horse-hair or any stuffing available. The skirts of the doublets varied from the very short, virtually hidden by the girdle, flared, standing out to cover the join between doublet and the stuffed hose, or in a separate scalloped border slit into tabs. Double skirts were not uncommon, the over skirt being fastened at the armhole by buttons and the join at the shoulder hidden by small rolls of padding called 'wings'. These wings were made of the same material as the doublet and worn throughout the period. The sleeves were made either narrow and close-fitting to the wrist, fastened up with a dozen buttons or leg-of-mutton shape known as 'trunk' sleeves which were pinked and slashed. Usually worn about the 1575s with the false hanging sleeves. The wider sleeves were always padded and stiffened, bombast was the name given to all types of stuff-

Monk in the typical hooded habit with belt and purse c 1600

25

ing, this was typical of the age.

The girdle was made from either leather, gold, silver, silk or velvet. Decorations ranged from embossing of leather with hangers to support either a sword or dagger, to precious and semi-precious stones.

...let with slight peascod... with narrow skirt. Small laced ruff from high collar. Full slashed trunks. Bonnet with feather   c 1570

Man in a doublet with a short skirt. High close fitting ruff with a short just below waist cloak. Short round hose with canions and high stockings with ribbon fastenings   c 1600

The *jerkin* (or jacket) was usually unpadded and worn over the doublet, it was fitted with either a low or high standing collar, fastened from the collar to the waist. The skirt was either short and followed the contours of the doublet, or was long almost reaching the bottom of the hose. The jerkin

A man in a bombasted doublet of the Spanish fashion, slightly peascod with a short skirt. It was slashed and pinked with a standing collar and a small ruff. The short trunk hose were padded and slashed. He has a short hip length cape and a tall flat topped hat. The boy is dressed in a close fitting doublet with full sleeves from the wings. High necked with a small closed ruff. He is wearing the German type barret hat decorated with feathers   c 1590

was more frequently without sleeves, sometimes with only a short puff sleeve with or without the real or false hanging sleeves. In the 1580s it was considered very fashionable to wear just one sleeve of the jerkin and to leave the other hanging loosely. The 'buff jerkin' or leather jerkin made from oiled ox-hide, was in reality a military fashion adopted for civilian fashion.

The *gown* which had been in fashion since about the middle of the fifteenth century was now used in ceremonial, or professional occupations by the older men for warmth over the doublet or as a négligée at home.

Soldier wearing leather winged jerkin over a shirt. Metal gorget round neck. Full knee length breeches and stockings. Tall crowned hat. A gunner of 1588

Buff jerkin with ribbon points. High crowned hat with feather c 1580

Doublet and bombasted trunk hose   c 1577

Man dressed in open doublet worn over a chemise. Trunk hose, called 'Pluderhosen', were voluminous, so made to be hitched up to give a baggy effect across the middle   c 1570

Outdoor wear   Cloaks and capes were the height of fashion until the beginning of the seventeenth century. The short Spanish cape was the most popular, this was fitted with a hood, it was usually deep and pointed, trimmed with buttons and loops, fitted with a small turn down collar. Due to the short length of this cape it could be worn either over one or both shoulders. The French cloak (manteau à la reître) was long, reaching the ankles, and very full, an ideal garment for travelling. The Dutch cloak was again short and full about waist length, fitted with wide sleeves. The cloak or cape was an essential part of the fashionable man's costume. It was considered to be a mark of social superiority, even to the wearing of them at home.

Another military dress turned civilian fashion was the 'mandilion'; this was a loosely fitting hip length jacket and hanging sleeves with wings. The vertical side slits made a back and front panel. It was pulled on over the head, and buttoned from the standing collar to the chest only. The mandilion was worn rather strangely in a sideways fashion, with the panels draped over the shoulders, with the sleeves hanging down, back and front.

Neckwear   The most characteristic fashion of this period was the ruff. The small ruff either attached to the shirt or separate was frequently worn open at the throat. The medium ruff was closed all round. The cartwheel ruff was large and closed all round. To support the latter was the 'underpropper' or 'supportasse' a wire framework attached to the doublet collar and the ruff pinned to it. From the simple goffered band the ruff grew to become double, treble or even more layers, becoming more complex with the introduction of starch in the 1560s. Poking sticks were used to create the tubular pleats.

Trunk hose   The term 'hose' was used to indicate breeches. 'Trunk hose' were the popular garments of the period, padded and covering the thighs and in one with the stockings, later the term referred only to the breeches part. The two styles were usually slashed and from the slashing a contrasting colour was visible. Canions or leg coverings filling in the space between the trunk hose and the stockings, were also worn. The German trunkhose or 'pluderhosen' were popular from about mid-century and had large slashing profusely stuffed with coloured silks spilling over the edges. They were

Formal overgarment gown with short puffed sleeves and kick-up shoulders worn over a bodice and skirt with a small neck ruff c 1569

Elizabethan soldier in a leather winged jerkin with loose breeches tied at the knees. A tall rounded hat with upturned brim c 1572

usually knee-length but often longer.

Breeches with separate stockings came in various styles, Venetian, which fastened just below the knee, were either skin tight with the stockings pulled up over them and gartered above the knee, or gathered in at the waist and padded round the hips. Popular was the 'Venetian voluminous' type with the pickadil border at the knees. The terms used were many and varied, such as trunk slops, French hose, Spanish slops, full slops, trunks, etc. The word slops meaning usually without padding. Tailored stockings were popular

Wide brimmed decorated hat
c 1607

English type tall bonnet   c 1575

Bonnet with ear pieces   c 1585

Bonnet with feather   c 1575

until the end of the sixteenth century, thereafter knitted stockings became the vogue.

Footwear   Garters of silk ribbon and taffeta trimmed with diamonds and jewels of all descriptions were usually tied just below the knees, holding the stockings in place. Plain buckled straps were worn and fastened just below the knee, with the stockings rolled back completely hiding the strap. The stockings were clocked (embroidered) in various patterns. The names 'Nether stocks' referred to the stockings which met the breeches at the knees and 'upperstocks' to the breeches.

Men's shoes were generally round toed, with low wedge heels making their appearance towards the end of the century. The high heel of the low-cut shoe decorated with a large shoe rose was only for the ultra-fashionable. Shoes were made close to the ankle with the uppers long and ending in two small tongues, these were often fastened with straps, or sometimes with thread through an eyelet hole. The uppers were usually slashed or pinked into a design. Pumps were also worn at this time by both sexes. The high-dress boots for riding in the late 1580s were turned down to just below the knee, the tops being scalloped, after 1590 they became popular walking boots. Leggings were made to protect the stockings, these were called 'cockers'.

Headwear   Hats were worn both in and out of doors. The flat hat, a small round beret type with a narrow brim, decorated with a feather, was popular until about the 1570s. As the century progressed the crowns became higher like a high crowned bowler, and all hats, whether high, low or flat crowned were made in leather, beaver, velvet or felt. Hats were trimmed with ribbon hat bands, or with gold, silver, pearl or crystal buttons, and decorated with feathers. Decorative under-caps were worn, these were sometimes referred to as night caps for which they were used.

Hair   The *hair styles* generally throughout Europe were the same. The hair being cropped all over, was brushed up away from the forehead and stuck with the aid of gum, as also was the moustache and cropped beard, this fashion lasted to the end of the sixteenth century. From about the 1590s came the longer hair styles reaching the shoulders. The love-lock, a tress of hair, very long and plaited with a ribbon

A man in short trunk hose with canions, doublet with peascod belly and a narrow skirt. The armour followed the shape of the doublet with the added tassets in front. A ruff encircled the neck. The lady is in a close fitting bodice with a stomacher. The décolletage is filled in with a neckscarf. The sleeves are straight with slashings at the elbows. The full skirt over the petticoat. A large feather hat c 1580

Gentleman in Venetian trunk hose with the stockings drawn over them. The slashed doublet has a peascod belly and full slashed bishop sleeves without wings. He wore a large cartwheel ruff. The lady wore the bodice with a long stomacher over the French farthingale style petticoat. The bodice had straight sleeves with turned back lace cuffs. She had a lace fan shaped ruff. In her hand she had a folding fan   c 1580

The man wears a close fitting doublet with long straight sleeves. Over the doublet he wears a military gorget, back and front plates of armour. Both doublet and armour has a slight peascod shape. The short trunk hose were bombasted and paned.

tied at the end, was brought forward to hang over the chest and became very fashionable. The wearing of beards was fashionable throughout the period, the Vandyke, Pickdevant, Spade beard, Square and Marquisetto are but a few of the types worn. Wigs, patches and make-up were worn only by the dandies of the period.

Gloves Elbow-length gauntlet *gloves* of silk and velvet and gold fringed, were often slashed at the fingers to reveal the rings worn on the fingers. The wearing of one glove and carrying the other was practised throughout Europe. Perfumed gloves imported from France and Spain were fashionable as were the doeskin ones for riding.

The boy is wearing the Venetian trunk hose reaching just over the knees. The doublet is winged and sleeveless. The sleeves of the undergarment are straight ending with a small cuff which matched the small close ruff around his neck. He wore a high crowned bonnet with feathers   c 1577

Handkerchiefs were usually carried in the hand, these were still a luxury and were trimmed with lace and were made in cambric, silk, lawn or velvet. Carried by men were the leather or silk purses, slung from the girdle. A sword was supported with hangers from the girdle. The dagger was slung in a horizontal position behind the right hip. A gorget or military steel collar was frequently worn as part of civilian fashion.

Masks were worn which covered the whole face and made from velvet or silk worn only to conceal identity.

Jewellery Neck chains, miniatures and bracelets were worn and carried by members of the court.

Elizabethan clown costume usually parti-coloured. The scalloped tunic sleeves were tipped with little brass bells. The chaperon cap and bell hood had a coxcomb on the top. The scalloped neck piece and the hanging head pieces were also tipped with brass bells. He wore long tied soft leather shoes and carried a short stick with coloured ribbons and a 'fool's head' c 1603

James I 1603-1625 — Charles I 1625-1649 —The Commonwealth 1649-1660

In the first quarter of the seventeenth century no European country held sway as leaders of fashion. The Dutch burghers, however, temporarily became the imitated fashion, due to their great commercial wealth and their dislike of the Spanish rulers. Whereas the Spanish fashion had tended to divide the body with hips and shoulders greatly emphasised; Dutch costume, in contrast, made everything in one, giving a full round shape with comfort and a freedom of movement.

This was an era of turmoil and change. France was presided over by Cardinal Richelieu and subsequently by Mazarin; Germany was attacked by the leading powers, England was in a state of rebellion and finally Civil War. The Pilgrim Fathers landed in New England.

France had made the greatest changes in fashion and by 1625 had completely changed the silhouette of both male and female. Gone was the bombast and stiffness and into fashion came all the soft folds and draperies. Cast aside was the farthingale and stomacher, adopted was the high waist-line, loose falling skirts, lace and ribbons replacing the precious stones and the whalebone.

With certain reservations, the courts of Europe began by about 1630 to accept the French influence of costume. The noticeable exceptions being that of Spain and Portugal who clung tenaciously to their own styles of dress.

This was an era of Puritans and Cavaliers, each displaying their modes of life by their mode of fashion. The Baroque style, which had begun in Italy as far back as the 1550s, now began to infiltrate into Northern Europe, first in architecture then into fashion.

The sumptiousness of the Baroque style became apparent towards the middle of the seventeenth century. France took the lead in art and fashionable costume, and art and crafts-manship flourished. Paris became the fashion centre with organised publicity; each month two full-sized dolls dressed in the latest fashion were sent to London, and later to other European capitals. These were *Les Poupées Fameuses*.

This was an era of Cavalier versus Puritan or rather French fashion versus Dutch modes, and in each country the battle

Clergyman in the habit and headwear of a Cardinal, worn in the period c 1600

The lady is wearing a Dutch fashion bodice with a low décolletage and spreading band collar. The sleeves are wrist length with a turned back lace cuff. The full skirt is covered with a long apron in the front. The coif is close fitting over the ears. The gentleman is wearing a close fitting unstiffened doublet with the skirt tabs overlapping. He wears long slops which are caught at the knees with ribbon ties. He has a falling band collar and three-quarter cloak   c 1630

French king's bodyguard, musketeer, wearing a tabard. The laced collar went high to the neck. Large slouched turned-up hat with feather. High leather boots and gauntlets   c 1628

was fought. With the Restoration in England after the Civil War and Commonwealth, the victory was conceded to French fashion which went to an extravagant extreme. During this period the development of men's fashion was more intriguing than women's fashion. The masculine soldierly costumes were generally replaced by effeminate male clothing. The excessive trimmings of ribbon loops on the stiff wide Rhinegrave breeches gave the ludicrous effect of petticoats.

One of the most important innovations of the French fashion is this period was the wig. By 1660 the wig became the symbol of the aristocracy, it typified the ruling classes. Wigmaking reached such a stage of perfection that the perruque makers of France were in demand all over Europe. Gradually wigs replaced natural hair, the latter being shaven off or cut very close to the head. The demand for wigs of

Cardinal de Richelieu shown in his armour and high leather boots which he wore with his clerical robes at the Siege of La Rochelle, 1628

Soldier in a buff leather coat with a lobster tail pot helmet, breast and back plates of armour. A carbine on a swivel belt and powder flask. High bucket boots turned down. The lady has the

high waisted fashion bodice with a deep basque and a pointed stomacher. Three-quarter sleeves with a deep lace cuff, a wide deep bertha collar and a long full skirt   c 1645

Large cocked hat   c 1620

human hair was so great and so expensive, that wigs of wool, horsehair or goathair were made. By the end of the century wigs were at their most elaborate. The full bottomed wig was a cascading mass of curls, which was arranged in peaks either side of the centre parting, falling over the shoulders, continuing down the back to the waist. Women wore the long wig curls, but never reached the splendour of the male wig. The female answer to the high male wig was the wearing of the 'fontange' which was tier upon tier of wired upstanding lace or ribbon, reaching its greatest height by 1699 then became smaller reducing to two tiers and became

The lady is wearing a high waisted gown. The bodice has a deep basque and stomacher and is sleeveless. The full sleeves of the chemise are seen. The deep bertha collar surrounds the low décolletage. The skirt is full and trained. A fur muff is carried. The gentleman has a short close fitting doublet with sleeves long to the wrist. The long legged breeches are unconfined at the knees with a ribbon waistband. A falling band collar encircles the neck. Bucket type top boots are worn. The three-quarter length cape is worn over the shoulders. A wide brimmed hat with feathers   c 1646

Cardinal de Richelieu in his full habit and cloak of red c 1635

known as the 'commode', later becoming a mere lace cap.

In the 1680s the extravagant extremes of the Baroque became a little more serene, being replaced by a more elegant splendour and dignity. Making their appearance for the first time was the forerunner of the modern male suit, the coat or 'justaucorps', the waistcoat and the breeches. The long, loose-fitting jacket or casaque was knee-length with large turned back sleeves and was originally part of the soldier's uniform; it was taken up by the fashionable civilian but shaped closer to the body. The breeches became narrow fitting knee breeches or culottes, whilst the doublet underneath was lengthened to a knee-length waistcoat.

The fashionable silhouette was the accent on slimness and imposing dignity. Gone were the ribbon fineries for the male. The long waistcoats although of coloured brocades, as were the narrow breeches, were less colourful and were

The lady is wearing a high waisted basqued bodice with a stomacher front. It has a laced bertha over the low décolletage. The overskirt is hitched up at the sides to reveal the petticoat. The gentleman is wearing a jerkin with wings over which is worn breast and back plate armour. The sleeves are slit down the seam through which can be seen the shirt sleeves. He is wearing the cloak-bag breeches fringed with ribbon points. He has a sash around the waist and has a wide brimmed hat with feathers   c 1640

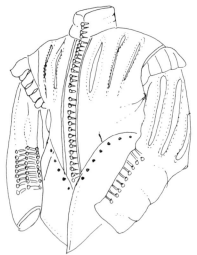

Slashed doublet with high neck piece   c 1625

generally made of material matching the coat. The cravat had completely taken over from the lace collars and ruffs. The most well known at this period was the 'Steinkirk' which was a loosely tied scarf of lace or lawn with the ends twisted into the shirt front or drawn through a ring. The name derived from the Battle of Steenkerque in 1692, when the French cavalry charged and caught the opposing army with their dress in disorder as they were taken by surprise.

Women's fashions followed the slimmer fashionable silhouette of the men. Dresses lengthened into a train, revealing the underskirt or jupe. The drapery gathered at the back was supported by a frame, making the first bustle effect. Embroidery became very popular once again, but with the Baroque strong formal shapes, with richness and splendour.

Women's costume   For the first half of the seventeenth century there were two styles: the old, that of the Spanish fashion with some modifications, and the new, under Dutch and French influence.

Bodice The old style was composed of the bodice and petticoat, the gown remaining a separate part of the costume, which could be worn with or without a farthingale.

The low necked bodice remained in vogue with the long tapering waist, which was sometimes edged with a narrow doublet skirt which was of scalloped tabs. The fastenings were down the front, by buttons or lacing or left as a V-shaped gap which was covered by a stomacher. The stomacher being so placed to give an extreme décolletage cut below the bosom, which was a fashion for unmarried women or as a sign of maidenhood. The high-necked bodice was worn without the stomacher, fastening down the front with buttons or lacing and closed round the neck with a closed ruff. The trunk sleeves were full at the top with a kick-up effect at the shoulder; then narrowed towards the wrist where they were fastened with buttons and finished with small turned-back cuffs or hand ruffs. Large hanging sleeves, usually false, were sometimes added. Tight fitting sleeves were worn, usually open down the seam and fastened by a ribbon at the elbow, which in turn revealed the partlet sleeves below.

The *jacket* or doublet was fashionable in the first quarter of the century, this was the forerunner of the riding jacket, it was a type of bodice without padding, very close-fitting and flared from the waist. It was collarless and was cut to a wide V or U shape in front, sometimes revealing the bosom. The sleeves fitted the arms closely and fastened at the wrist with buttons and then ornamented with lace cuffs. The shoulders were always fitted with wings.

The *skirt* depended very much on the structure of the nether garments, be they farthingale or petticoats, usually being ankle length, revealing the high heeled satin shoes.

Bodice From 1625 the newer styles began to evolve and the ruff and farthingale began to disappear. The bodice became short-waisted giving a higher waistline effect, and was made with or without a basque. The basque bodice was similar in cut to the male doublet with tabs which were deep and square. The bodice had both back and front fastening, but

Middle class fashion with pulled back skirt revealing the petticoat. Large wide collar and cuffs. High crowned hat was worn over a laced coif   c 1645

more often laced at the back. The neckline was a very low décolletage, either square or round. The bodice without basques was tight-fitting to the waist which came to a point in the front, it was stiffened with whalebone. The neck was similar to the basque bodice. Both garments had a narrow sash, or belt, which followed the waistline and tied into a bow.

The ladies are wearing the chaperon type head covering and deep bertha collars. The lady on the left wears her overskirt hitched up all round revealing the petticoat and the lady on the right has the overskirt bunched up at the back (bustle fashion). Fur muffs are carried by both   c 1640

A townswoman with a close fitting sleeved bodice with her overskirt drawn up all round revealing the petticoat. She is wearing a deep shoulder length bertha collar edged in lace and a high crowned hat with a wide brim   c 1640

Dutch close fitting coif with cartwheel ruff   c 1635

Wide brimmed hat with feather decoration   c 1620

Centre parting with massed curls and ringlets either side c 1628

Sleeves were full or ballooned and paned below and above the elbow, finishing at the wrist with lingerie cuffs matching the drooping collar. The skirt was loosely gathered at the waist, softly falling into irregular folds reaching the ground. The elongated inverted V opening in the front revealed the petticoat which was often of the same colour and material. By about the mid-30s the closed skirt became more popular.

The *négligée* or nightgown was popular, but was not, as its name implies, used as night attire. On the contrary, it was worn during the day for both formal and informal functions. It was a gown without the stiffened under-bodice and was in vogue throughout the century.

Neckwear   Ruffs continued well into the century, with many variations. The later styles like the 'broad bertha' which was a falling band or wide collar which reached from neck to shoulder in depth, with names like gorget, neckerchief and rebato. Hand ruffs went out of fashion in the early 30s and the turned back cuff became the most popular term. Materials for all neck and wrist wear was linen, lawn, or laced borders. The borders were usually vandyked.

Outdoor wear   Worn mainly for travelling was the cloak, which was long to the ground, with a flat large turned-down collar; fastened at the neck by a cord. The cloaks were often fur lined. Popular was the tippet or short cape which reached to just below the waist. When made in lace it was worn as a négligée. The safeguard, as its name implies, was a skirt worn over the gown skirt to protect it from dirt whilst riding.

Loose outer short coats were worn. These reached to just below the hips and were edged and lined with fur for the winter, popularly known as Dutch jackets.

Although *headwear* was popular it was fashionable to be bare headed both indoors as well as out. Again there was a great variety of headwear from the close-fitting French hood, the laced Mary Stuart hood, the bongrace, and the arched hood. The 'sugarloaf' hat with the tall crown was popular as also was the 'cavalier' hat.

Hair   The coiffure of the latter period was the fringe over the forehead and loose, short hanging curls on either side

43

The man on the left is wearing a loose winged doublet and false hanging sleeves. He has a short wrap-around cloak, high soft leather boots and a high crowned hat with feathers. The man on the right is wearing a loose fitting winged doublet with false sleeves. Short trunk hose and canions with high soft leather boots. His neck is encircled with a wide ruff   c 1660

44

Side ringlets to shoulder length with front hair brushed back c 1660

of the face, with a flat bun at the back of the head. The hair was usually decorated with bows of ribbon, plumes of lace pieces. Hair jewellery was going out of fashion except at court.

Beauty aids   Paint and powder were also fashionable as were perfumes and patches.

Accessories   *Shoes* and *stockings* were similar to the men's wear, with the exception of hats.

Gloves were always worn or carried. By the mid-century long gloves began to appear, with ribbons worn at the elbow over the glove to prevent it from slipping down.

The handkerchiefs similar to the men's were usually edged with lace, and were always carried.

Short *scarves* were worn as also were the chin-clouts or mufflers. The latter being squares of material diagonally folded and worn over the mouth and chin.

Masks were worn as protection against being recognised and for the beauty of the complexion, were either full face masks, held in place by a button which was attached to the inside and held between the teeth, or a half mask covering the upper part of the face and held by ties fastened at the back of the head.

Large feather *fans* with ornate handles were carried, as also were small tasselled purses.

Jewellery   Although necklaces, bracelets and jewellery in general were worn, the lavish use of jewellery ceased to be fashionable, and bejewelled dress embroidery virtually ceased altogether by mid-century.

Women I660-1715

For *women*, from the middle of the seventeenth century, the bodice, boned and close fitting was again long waisted, coming to a deep point in front. The horizontal low-cut neck-line encircled the bosom, baring the shoulders, it was edged by the lace of the partlet or chemise and below by a deep lace 'bertha'.

Lady in a Court dress with a page. Closed close fitting bodice with round décolletage and long train   c 1700

The stomacher continued to be worn, this being embroidered or ornamented with 'échelles', an arrangement of ribbon loops down the centre.

Sleeves varied from being full to the elbow, gathered into a band from which emerged the full frilled sleeve of the chemise, to the short straight sleeve ending just above the elbow and trimmed at the lower edge with lace or ribbon loops.

The skirt was gathered in at the waist and hung loosely to the ground, the front was usually open, revealing the

The lady is in a deep pointed bodice with short puffed sleeves with full cuffs ending at the elbows. The overskirt is hitched up to reveal the underskirt. She is wearing the corkscrew curl hairstyle. The gentleman is wearing a short jacket with slit open sleeves showing the shirt sleeves beneath with a deep laced cuff. He is wearing the petticoat beneath, the front edges were either folded back and secured or allowed to fall normally to the ground. A 'Cul-de-Paris' or bustle was worn and the overskirt was gathered up behind.

Dutch type skirt breeches with ribbon loops around the waist. A deep falling band collar surrounds the neck   c 1665

47

The gentleman is wearing a doublet with a military gorget. He is wearing full knee breeches secured below the knees. The full top boots are over them. He is carrying the wide brimmed cavalier type hat. The lady is wearing a high waisted bodice tied at the waist by a ribbon sash. The full sleeves are drawn in above the elbow. A flat collar surrounds the low décolletage. The skirt is long and full c 1638

48

The man on the left is dressed in the style of 1628 with the unpadded doublet, trunk hose and canions. The lady is wearing the popular farthingale of 1603, the bodice is close-fitting to the waist with a low décolletage. The fashionable man to the right is dressed in a masquerade costume with a full face mask. The trunk hose are the 'plunder hosen' variety of 1578

The man on the left is in a close fitting coat with full button decoration, and with 'bloomer' type breeches, 1684. In the centre is a flamboyantly dressed artisan in a short jerkin leather coat, doublet and hose with codpiece and high soft leather boots, 1575. The lady is in the fashion of 1630 with the low décolletage and fan shaped high collar, balloon shaped sleeves, and stiffened stomacher, open-robed style revealing the petticoat

Bodice   From about 1680 the close-fitting bodice of the gown style was popular, the bodice being joined to a full gathered trained skirt, open in the front. The neckline was either square or round edged, with a border which came over the shoulders forming a V at the waist where it was tied with a ribbon or belt. The gap was filled with an embroidered stomacher.

The *sleeves* were usually short, plain and straight; ending just above the elbow, the frilled sleeve of the chemise hung below. Later either single or multiple frills were attached.

The underskirt, or *petticoat*, was slightly shorter than the gown and sometimes trained. It came in various patterns, such as flounces, fringes, embroidery and quilting.

The *négligée* or 'mantua', although similar to the gown was somewhat looser and used mainly as a wrap, this was often referred to as a 'nightgown', although it was worn for most informal occasions, it was also worn at the theatre. As its name implies, it was made in the first instance from mantua silk, and was of a dark colour or black.

Low décolletage dress   c 1660

49

Coats similar to the men's fashion were worn for both horse-riding and walking. Very fashionable was the tippet which was waist-length, usually double, the upper cape forming a deep collar, and made in fur or velvet. The 'pallatine' was merely a tippet of fur with two dangling ends in front. From the 1680s onwards long broad scarves were worn, these could be shoulder deep and falling almost to the knees.

Lady and boy in Court dress. The lady has a gown with a trained overskirt hitched up and turned back bustle fashion revealing the petticoat. Off the shoulder décolletage, sleeves to elbow length showing full sleeves of the undergarment. Low fontange headdress. The boy is in a coat with deep cuffs. Armour breast plate and sash, carrying a three-cornered hat   c 1703

Coif with side lappets which hung down to waist level. Stiff laced front piece   c 1685

Headwear   As in the previous decade the wearing or not wearing of any form of headwear was still fashionable. The middle classes favoured the tall crowned wide brimmed hats. Most popular was the 'chaperones' or headkerchiefs, fastened on like a hood. The tall structural fontange, made up with multiple stiff frills of lace or linen, tier upon tier, was the most fashionable by the end of the century. Two floating lappets of linen or lace hung down behind; the front hair was twisted on to a wire frame or 'palisade' in front, onto which were sewn artificial ringlets. Hair dressed in this fashion was known as a coiffure à la Fontanges, after the Duchesse de Fontanges.

Hair styles remained very much the same until about the 1660s, then various styles became fashionable. Some had corkscrew curls massed on each side above the ears with the hair brushed back with a flat bun at the back. Others were combined with long ringlets crossing over the shoulders. Closed massed curls all over the head were also popular. Terms such as Crève-coeur, Confidants, Pasagère and Bergère were given to some form or other of curls. The hair was sometimes decorated with ribbon loops, ribbon bows and top knots, and jewelled hairpins were worn.

Beauty aids   Make-up was used extensively as were the mouches or black patches. Plumpers were usually light cork balls which were placed in the mouth to fill out the cheeks.

Footwear   Fine *shoes* tapering to a square about 25 mm (1 in.) wide, of beautifully embroidered fabrics were worn with a high 'Louis' heel. They were fastened by buckled straps over a high instep tongue. Pantofles or mules which were high-heeled were popular. Stockings of knitted wool or silk in bright colours were fashionable. Gloves and mittens in velvet, silk and lace were always worn, and elbow length gloves were worn for all formal and full dress occasions. Tall canes continued in fashion. Masks were still worn as a concealment of identity, either vizard masks, which covered the whole face or the Loo mask which covered only half the face.

Accessories were fans of rare beauty and designs, snuff-boxes and boutonnières (a small glass or tin which carried water for holding flowers). Muffs were still carried but tended to become a little smaller.

Men 1603-1660

For *men* this was an important period in costume, it was the last phase of the bombast and the abandonment of the peascod belly.

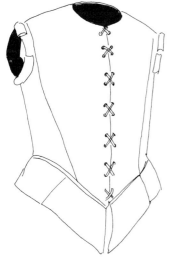

Short buff leather jerkin
c 1580

The *doublet* which earlier had the short skirt with overlapping tabs from now on had longer tabs which curved down in front to a point, making a long waisted effect, usually with a belly-piece. The waistline was studded with eyelet holes for the attachment of the breeches by lace ties. The doublet was fastened from the top of the collar to the waist, the high standing collar being fastened with loops. The sleeves usually plain and tight fitting were sometimes full at the top and paned at the shoulders and elbows from which they were fastened below with buttons almost to the wrist. The panes revealed the coloured lining. The projecting welts or wings encircled the shoulder joins. Although the sword belt which followed the curve of the waistline was fashionable it was generally replaced by the late 20s with a cross shoulder belt or a baldrick. By mid-century the doublet was high waisted and looser fitting. Gone was the padding with little or no stiffening. The tabbed skirt was now merely a border. The corseted shape was discarded and the doublet virtually became a waistcoat with sleeves. The sleeves and the upper part of the doublet was often padded revealing the lining or the shirt below. Sometimes the doublet was so short that a gap existed between doublet and breeches, which was bridged by the protruding shirt, the shirt now becoming of great importance, was made very full and loose in the body and sleeve. The collar, usually stiffened with buckram, supported the upright band of the standing or falling collar.

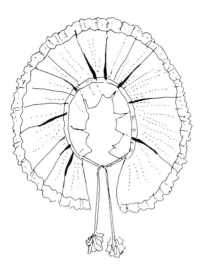

Falling band ruff   1620-1630

Jerkin   Popular was the buff coat or leather jerkin; this was of military origin and was close-fitting with a high waist line and a deep skirt which overlapped in the front, being slit at the back and sides, it had a round neck without a collar and buttoned down the front to the waist. It could be worn with close-fitting sleeves usually of another material, with hanging tubular sleeves or could be worn without sleeves. Coats and cloaks were worn, popular was the cassock coat, a wide loose coat flaring out towards the hem, which fastened down the front and often trimmed with buttons and ribbons, usually with just a rounded neck without a collar.

Cavalier in a slashed sleeved jerkin with ribbon rosettes and points. Large laced falling band collar. Three-quarter length cape was worn. Full breeches to below knees tied off with ribbon rosettes   c 1633

The lady has a close fitting bodice with a stomacher deep in the front. The open hanging sleeves show the chemise sleeves. The open overskirt shows the buttoned down the front petticoat. Around the low décolletage is a spreading standing band collar. She is wearing a tall high crowned hat with a turned up brim and feathers. The gentleman has a high waisted doublet with a deep skirt. The doublet is winged and buttoned down the front. The front seams of the undergarment are slit and buttoned. He has a broad falling band collar, oval breeches secured at the knees, and carries a full cloak

Falling band lace edged collar c 1630

In *neckwear* the small ruff was still worn and was generally being replaced by the newer large falling band. This distinct style in neckwear became very popular and fashionable and worn throughout Europe. The neckpieces were tied in front with band-strings which were white tasselled cords.

Also coming into fashion was a length of folded linen which was tied loosely round the neck, the ends usually ending in a lace finish, known as a cravat, this being the name given after the Croatian or Cravates soldiers serving with the French, who wore such a fashion to protect their throats. Wristwear followed the fashion of the collars both in style and material.

Breeches were in various forms and of various names such as venetian, galligaskins, slops, cloak bag breeches

Tall beaver hat   c 1638

Priest in skull cap and high collar   c 1658

An English officer in the loose coat fashion, buttoned from neck to hem. Elbow length sleeves with turned back cuffs revealing full shirt sleeves. A deep plain lawn falling band collar, wig and high cocked hat. A peasant girl of the period c 1670

and Spanish hose, generally the breeches were very full and unpadded and baggy at the knees, or were full at the top and moderately tight over the knees, where they were buttoned and decorated with bunches of ribbon loops. They were cut so that they were supported by the hips without attachments to any garment as previously.

Footwear   Tailored stockings, although still being worn, were now less fashionable than the knitted variety which were being worn by all classes. Garters were worn not only to secure the stockings but also to serve as decoration and usually were small sashes tied in bows just below the knee on the outer side, they were made in a variety of materials such as net, ribbon, silk, silver and gold cloth and fringed with gold braid.

Short leather boots with falling tops of a Spanish design became fashionable in the late 20s, these were in multi-colours, from beige to blue. Spurs became fashionable for walking, thus the spur leathers became larger in size and shape, and were worn both in and out of doors. Shoes with high red heels and red edged soles were in vogue and were worn with full dress and remained a court fashion until the end of the eighteenth century. The popular style of shoe had small side openings, the uppers finishing with a rounded tongue, fastening by shoe strings made of ribbon ties, often bunched the toe was usually square shaped. The long boots with the cup-shaped tops worn for both riding and walking were decorated with falling lace-edged, embroidered boot hose, stockings were worn between the boot and the silk stockings.

If the boot hose was not worn a separate embroidered flounce was tied to the knee and allowed to fall over the boot. Sometimes the boot cup was lined with elaborate lace frills.

Headwear of all types were worn indoors for all formal occasions including the partaking of meals. Fashionable was the Cavalier type, made from felt and beaver, it had a wide brim with a low crown. The copotain or sugar-loaf hat had a tall conical crown with brims of varying depth, either flat or slightly turned up. The hats were trimmed with decorative hat bands made from cord or ribbons, silk, buttons or jewelled ornamentation and with or without plumes. The use of beaver in the manufacture of hats became

French Soldier with a collarless coat and an embroidered sash around his middle, also a broad shoulder sword belt. Wide flaring stiff knee flapped bucket boots. Wig and wide cocked hat decorated with feathers. The lady is in a low décolletage enclosed by a broad bertha. Close fitting bodice with elbow length sleeves with full sleeves of undergarment protruding. Full overskirt bunched up to reveal the underskirt. The head is draped with a long shawl scarf. A cloth muff is carried. She is wearing a black beauty mask   c 1675

A monk with a cowl and cape made of coarse woollen material c 1620

the vogue due to the great export of the North American colonists, previously these had come from Flanders. The hair styles varied from the full bushy type to the long hair with the cadenette love-lock, a tress of hair grown long, usually curled which was brought forward from the nape of the neck to dangle over one shoulder. It was often tied with a ribbon bow. This fashion which had started in the 1590s began to disappear in the late 1650s.

Hair The face was usually clean-shaven, although moustaches and vandyke beards were still worn. Wigs, although worn, did not reach their popularity until the late 1660s, when they became a status symbol at court.

Accessories *Canes* with knobs of gold, silver or bone decorated with bunches of coloured ribbons were carried.

Gloves, handkerchiefs and purses were also carried.

Earrings, usually pearl, were commonly worn until about the 1660s.

Muffs were carried, increasing in size as the century progressed, they were either held in the hand or slung from a ribbon round the neck.

Following military fashion broad sashes tied round the waist or across the shoulders were worn, as also were the steel gorget and the baldrick or shoulder-belt.

Men 1660-1715

Coats The short doublet with skirt continued in fashion until the 1670s, thereafter it became a little longer, closer fitting and with plain skirts. The high standing collar was stiffened with buckram. The front slit on the sleeve was replaced without a slit and ended elbow length with a turned back cuff. Fastened from neck to waist with buttons. The cassock continued to be worn as an alternative to the buff coat, but after 1665 developed into an overcoat. From 1665 the doublet was replaced by the coat and waistcoat, retaining their names to the present day. The waistcoat or vest was close-fitting at the waist and collarless, with the skirt falling loosely to just below the knees, being fastened at the waist by a sash. The sleeves were short and loose fitting.

The surcoat, a loose coat with short sleeves was worn

Soldiers of the period in clothes following the style and cut of the prevailing fashion. The cross- belt, heavy swords, bucket boots and weapons being the symbol of the military   c 1699

58

The male country fashion, loose coat without a collar with pockets set low and horizontal.

Wide petticoat breeches. Neckcloth decorated with ribbon loops which also decorated his hat and shoes. Working class French peasant girl wearing a close fitting laced bodice with a skirt to ankle length. Elbow length bodice sleeves with turned-back cuffs. Shawl neckerchief and apron with a central pocket   c 1678

The gentleman wearing the deep cuffed open coat without waist-coat revealing a shirt with steinkirk neckwear. Stockings were worn over the knee breeches Turned up hat decorated with feathers. Lady in a gown with stomacher and trained skirt hitched up behind revealing the underskirt with a short apron. The sleeves of the bodice are three-quarter length with deep flounces. High fontange and long gloves   c 1693

60

A gentleman in short loose open doublet which reveals the protruding shirt. The full sleeves with the front slip showed the shirt sleeves below. Full breeches with a lace frill at the knee and bound at the waist with ribbon bunches. Three-quarter length cloak over both shoulders. The lady is wearing a close-fitting narrow waisted bodice with a decorative stomacher. The deep décolletage shaped with a V style border. The full gathered trained skirt is hitched up behind and at both sides. The head is covered with a large kerchief   c 1670-1680

Funnel shaped dress with a laced bodice front and Dutch style three-quarter length jacket with long sleeves turned back into a deep cuff. The gentleman is wearing a coat open to the waist to reveal the waistcoat. The sleeves are long with a deep cuff. A long three-quarter length cloak is worn. A full bottomed wig and low crowned hat with a wide brim is also worn   c 1670

over the vest, it was somewhat shorter than the vest and fastened at the top by a clasp.

By about the mid 1670s the coat which fitted at the shoulders, hung loosely down to just below the knees. The skirt had side slits or vents to the hips. The coat was collarless and was fastened from neck to hem by buttons, usually the coat was worn open. The pockets at first were both vertical and horizontal, but the vertical type were quickly discarded, the pockets were placed very low on the skirt to some 5 to 7 cm (2 to 3 in.) from the hem. The sleeves remained to just elbow length, ending with deep turned-back cuffs which were fastened to the sleeve by buttons. By the 1680s the coat was cut to become closer to the waist and the pockets placed higher on the skirt. The sleeves became longer, reaching almost to the wrist. The trimming of

Fashionable Dutch costume of the petticoat breeches style with a short doublet revealing the chemise beneath. The breeches or rhinegraves, with large wide legs were profusely decorated around the waist and seams with large ribbon loops. Stockings were worn, over which were worn stirrup hose with a large decorative top. The full sleeveless cloak was worn over the shoulders. The neck was encircled by a wide falling band. He wore a tall sugar loaf hat trimmed with ribbon loops c 1665

a shoulder-knot, a bunch of ribbon loops, was often worn on the right shoulder only. From 1690 onwards the coat became close-fitting and a definite waist-line effect was achieved by the skirt becoming fuller and flaring out.

Rhinegrave costume   c 1660

The *waistcoat* was virtually the same, as the coat included the pockets, the sleeves being longer were usually turned back over the coat sleeve cuff. Although the waistcoat could be worn without the coat as an alternative, it soon became apparent that the wearing of the waistcoat with a coat, for economic reasons, need not have the back panel in the expensive rich colours so a cheaper material was used, such waistcoats became known as 'cheats'. After 1690 the waistcoat became a little shorter and fastened only by a few buttons at the waist, the other buttonholes being false and merely decorative; the opening revealed the frilled shirt and cravat which was usually edged in lace. Waistcoats were often worn in bed for warmth.

Outdoor wear   The cloak now worn on both shoulders continued to be worn until the late 70s, becoming most unfashionable. Thereafter the cloak was generally replaced by the overcoat. The most popular overcoat being the Brandenburg from the Prussian city of that name; this coat, large, loose fitting and somewhat shapeless was only calf length, but otherwise similar to the cassock. A fashionable utility coat was the 'jump', a short, thigh length loose fitting jacket, which fastened down the front with a halfway slit or vent at the back.

Négligées   During this period men wore the nightgown and turbans as négligées. The nightgown or banyan became the informal dress; this long, loose coat at first made from cotton, later appeared in heavy brocades and silks, with contrasting linings, it varied in styles from being wide sleeved to the close-fitting sleeve, but nearly always in coloured figured or striped materials. The turban or nightcap gave a respite from the heat and weight whilst the wig was discarded. The fashion was brought about by the trading between Europe and the Oriental countries such as India, Arabia and Persia.

The broad lace bordered *neckwear* remained in fashion until the early 70s, then the cravat or neckcloth became the vogue, fashion varying usually only in the method of tying or the amount of material used. The steinkirk remained popular throughout the period from the 1690s.

Shirts   With the short sleeves of the coat, the shirt sleeves which were full, came into display, ending at the wrist in

64

a full frill, or ruffle.

The very wide open *breeches* remained in fashion until about the 1670s. The most fashionable, although worn mainly at court, were the Rhinegraves or petticoat pantaloons, the definite feature of this fashion was the very wide legs reaching to the knees, they were fastened at the pleated waistband and resembled a short divided skirt. They were lavishly ornamented with lace and ribbon loops; ribbon loops formed a fringe round the waist and deep cannons of lace hung down from the knees. This fashion lasted until 1678, then they were replaced by the closed breeches or Spanish hose, these being a loose wide knickerbocker, falling over the knees, gathered in a band and fastening either above or below the knee, these ended with ribbon loops or cannons.

By the 1690s the plainer knee-length close-fitting breeches came into vogue. These breeches were generally of a different material to the coat, and were fastened at the outer side of the knee with buttons or buckles.

Gentleman in a collarless coat fastened from neck to hem. Low pockets with flaps. Full sleeves and deep cuffs. Rolled up stockings over breeches. He is wearing a full bottomed wig over which is the three cornered hat braided and feathered c 1700

Naval officer wearing a leather buff coat with short sleeves revealing the full chemise sleeves. Worn over this is the upper breast and back piece body armour. Full wig c 1665

High dressed curls over pads and ringlets hanging either side c 1690

The gentleman is wearing a loose coat with elbow length sleeves. It is fastened from neck to hem with buttons. The full shirt sleeves with lace cuffs show beneath the coat sleeves. He is wearing a fashionable wig and high crowned hat decorated with feathers. His sash denotes him to be a military man. The lady is wearing an open robe with a stomacher. The bodice is close-fitting ending in a centre point. It has a low off the shoulder décolletage decorated with ribbons. The open overskirt reveals the petticoat c 1664

Footwear　　After the seventies shoes were usually black, brown being the colour for hunting only. The red heels and edges were now used by the nobility as court wear. Shoes were square-toed with high square heel with open sides until the 1680s then they became closed. High in front of the ankles was the square-tongued uppers, which on occasions hung down revealing a red lining. Up to 1680 the shoes were fastened by ribbon or lace bows, thereafter being superseded by small oval buckles then by large, square buckles, they became very fashionable when adorned with pearls and diamonds.

Boots came in various styles, after 1660 boots were usually used for horseback. Soft fitted boots or buskins fastened by buckles or buttons became fashionable although the heavy bucket-type boots were very popular. High leather leggings or spatter-dashes, shaped like a close-fitting boot were worn with shoes, the joining of legging and shoe being covered by spur leathers. This was the forerunner of the popular gaiter. Footwear worn in this period were galoshes, clogs, pattens and for indoors mules and pumps. The military wore mainly the bucket boots with the wide stiff flaps which covered the knees, high heeled, square-toed with leather blocks above the heel for spurs.

The wearing of boot hose or long stockings with ornamental tops was popular until the 1680s. The most fashionable were the stirrup hose, which came high above the knee with decorative tops which, when turned down over the garter worn at the knee, fell deeply over the boot tops, these were very much in vogue during the Rhinegrave period.

Headwear　　The high sugar-loaf hat remained in popularity until the 1670s. Thereafter the low round crowned hat with a wide brim which could be cocked in various positions and fastened by buttons and loops became fashionable, this was decorated with ribbons or feathered plumes.

From 1690 onwards came the tricorne hat, cocked into a triangle with the point in front, usually trimmed with feather tips along the braided edge, later the tricorne was ornamented with uncurled ostrich plumes. The gentlemen's hats ceased to be worn indoors from about 1680.

The *hair* was worn long to the shoulders and the unfashionable wore their own hair dressed to resemble the more fashionable wig style.

Gentleman's full bottomed wig
c 1680

Simple wig style   c 1661

Full bottomed wig   c 1688

Wigs grew larger as the century progressed, becoming artificial in appearance, and made in mixtures of human and horse hair, which proved better for curling. Up to 1675 the wig was a mass of irregular curls which framed the face, and fell round the shoulders. Usually two front curls on either side were tied with ribbons. A more even distribution of curls became fashionable up to the 1690s and thereafter the huge full-bottomed wig or French wig became the fashion. The travelling wig or campaign wig was worn from about 1675 onwards, it was much shorter and ended in one or two corkscrew curls, being tied into a queue at the back. Both hair dyes and hair powder were in fashionable use. To avoid disturbing the wig the hat was carried.

Moustaches and beards from 1650 onwards were not considered fashionable, so most men were usually clean-shaven. The baldrick or shoulder belt which carried a small sword was long, wide and sometimes very ornate, being made of leather, embroidered silk or velvet, this fashion lasted until 1700. The dress-sword which emerged from the coat skirt was attached by a braid loop fastened to the vest, the sword was ornamented with bowknots or tasselled cords.

Accessories   Gloves of all types were either worn or carried from the fringed gauntlet gloves to the long elbow type.
Handkerchiefs which were tasselled or buttoned with lace edging were fairly large and were either carried in the hand or hung from a pocket.
Muffs were large and made from beautiful fur, satin or velvet and were carried by men in the winter time, attached by a ribbon round the neck or suspended from a ribbon belt round the waist.
The wearing of *jewellery* became less fashionable for men.
For affectation, mirrors, combs and snuff-boxes were carried.

STAGE PROPERTIES

Infantry sergeant wearing a leather jerkin with slashed at the seams sleeves. Oval trunk hose with below the knee ribbon ties. A large slouched hat with a turned up brim   c 1632

The most naturally accepted of 'theatre' are the properties. If these convey a sense of artistic authenticity the audience seems satisfied. From earliest days, properties existed, although stage sets and lighting were merely figments of the imagination — in fact they were purely vocal.

The property department is still an important, complex and fascinating part of the theatre. The complexity stems from the many art skills needed to produce most of the requirements necessary for any stage production.

The furnishing of the stage in the required period and the general paraphernalia of the set are just a part of the property department. Essential costume, accessories and hand properties are also the responsibility of 'props' both in the supplying and making of these articles.

In this chapter I have outlined all the items which would be used during this period for historical plays, including the arms and armour of the soldiers which prevailed during these troubled times of wars, rebellion and counter rebellion. The making of these specialised articles I must leave with the individuals responsible and hope that their ingenuity and skill will produce an authentic stage 'prop'.

Furniture   The Elizabethan and Jacobean period furniture was usually heavy and made from oak. England was the last to follow the Renaissance architecture and furniture. Thus it is permissible to include the old, heavy, ponderous Gothic-style furniture in Early Elizabethan plays. Later in the century the furniture became the over-ornate Renaissance models, which at this period were somewhat massive and profusely decorated.

The chest (an important and popular piece of furniture in stage dressings) developed from the crude plain wooden Gothic type to an ornate framed and panelled, almost elegant piece of furniture.

69

(a)

(b)

(c)

(d)

(e)

(f)

70

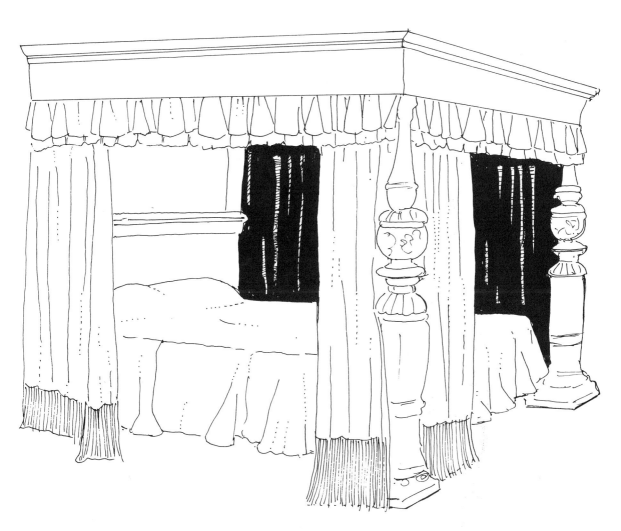

A curtained bed can dominate a scene. These should be studied, although basically the same, they varied in height and ornamentation

Drinking utensils of the period (a-b) Drinking mug (c) Ornate jug (d) Jug (e) Goblet (f) Candle snuffers

There was a great variety of cupboards changing in form and in function. The standing cupboard used in halls and dining rooms was a very large ornamented piece. Smaller ones were used as repositories, often in the bedroom. Later came the buffet which was used from the time of Elizabeth up to the Restoration. This displayed the crockery and had drawers.

The Renaissance chairs were straight rigid-backed and upholstered in fabrics of stamped leather, velvets, brocades and secured by braid. The Gothic/Renaissance chairs however, remained in fashion and were ornamental and uncomfortable, usually the box type.

With the advent of the farthingale, a chair was designed which was made without arms and had a low back with a narrow seat. The chairs were upholstered and the padded

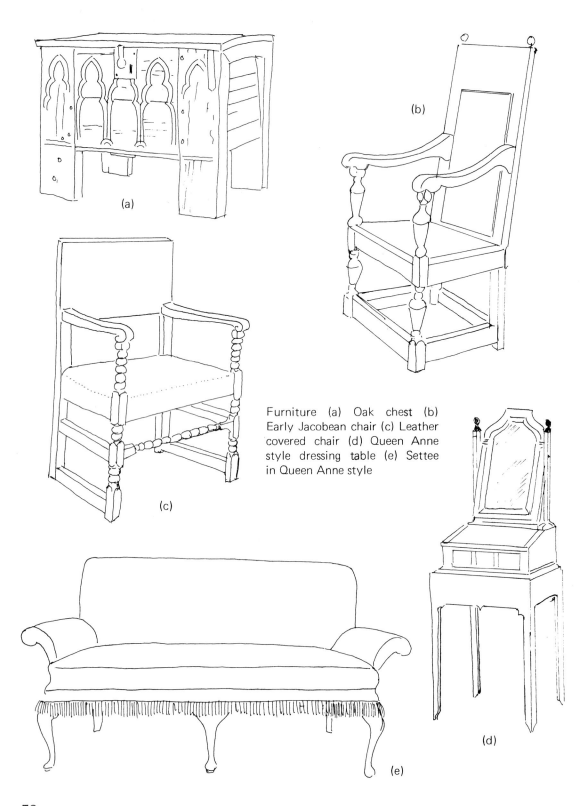

Furniture (a) Oak chest (b) Early Jacobean chair (c) Leather covered chair (d) Queen Anne style dressing table (e) Settee in Queen Anne style

The man on the left is a fashionable military officer. The sash which encircles the waist could also be worn over the left shoulder. The lady is in the fashion of 1640 with the broad décolletage and basqued bodice. The man is in the fashion of 1698 in close fitting coat, full breeches and large 'cocked at back only' hat

The man on the left is in the sombre fashion of the Spanish court style of the early seventeenth century. The lady is in the fashion of the 1690s with the long trained skirt and embroidered stomacher, and the 'bonnet a la Fontanges' headwear. On the right is a fashionable gentleman in the costume of 1660, known as the petticoat breeches style

An Infantry soldier with a leather jerkin and loose breeches caught at the knees, and leather high boots and a metal cabasset helmet c 1620

back tilted away from the upright.

More commonly used were stools, benches and forms. Tables were used in the large dining halls, these were large and heavy, gradually, however, during the period they became smaller in size. The Elizabethan draw-leaf or draw-top table with its large chunky bulbous type legs also lost favour and was replaced by smaller types with gate-legs. These were later made in a wide variety of styles and types, with the number of legs varying from four to twelve.

The most important and the most costly in its ornamental magnificence was the bed. The beds were usually four-poster, although the trestle type was also widely used. The four-poster was very large, the bed itself was a low frame on low small posts. But this was joined to a heavy carved bed framing two posts at the head and two further posts at the foot which were almost 3 m high (just over 9 ft.), to support the returns of the corniced testers. The corners of this were supported by solid carved columns. To this was attached heavy, richly embroidered tapestry, velvet or silk, fringed or edged, according to the wealth of the owner.

The walls throughout the period were decorated with hanging tapestries of velvet, brocade and silk, A cheaper version was a painted cloth of a canvas material with heraldic, religious or mythological subjects. Or cheaper still the paintings were on the plaster wall itself. Candles were the usual form of illumination, held in pewter or silver candlesticks. Tall candle stands of some 3 m (9 ft.) high which held several candles were often used, as were the chandelier type which hung suspended from the ceiling.

Mirrors other than the hand variety were not made in great quantity as glass and mirror-making had not reached a high degree of manufacture at this time, and only the wealthier houses displayed them. They were mainly imported into Europe via Venice which was the centre of the glass-making trade.

Kitchen utensils during this period were made from wood, pewter, iron and earthenware. The dressing of the stage would consist of such articles as cauldrons, pots (various shapes and sizes), skillets, frying pans, barrels, tubs, sieves, fire implements (pokers, shovels, etc), flesh hooks, ladles, skimmers, chafing dishes, mortar and pestle, knives and axes.

(a)

(b)

(c)

(d)

(e)

Furniture (a) Velvet covered fringed chair (b) Oak stool (c) Oak stool (d) Oak form (e) Oak chest

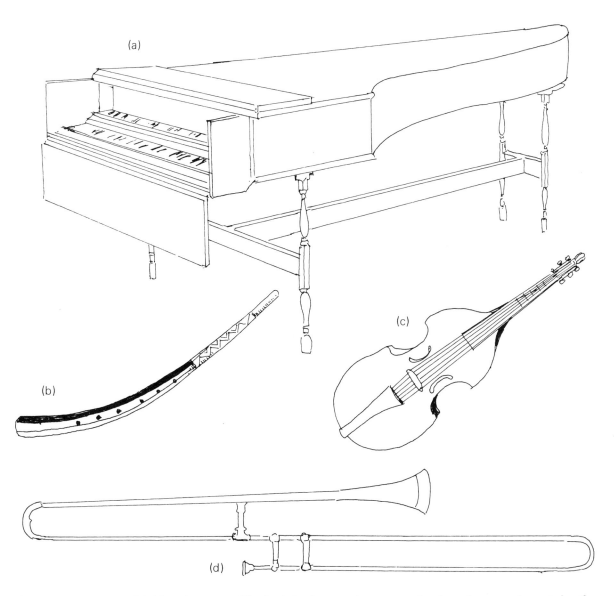

Musical instruments (a) Harpsichord late seventeenth century (b) Treble cornette, early seventeenth century (c) Viol, seventeenth century (d) Trombone, late seventeenth century

Musical instruments as usual played a great part in the lives of the people of this period. One of the most popular and familiar of instruments was the lute. Its design is so suited to its acoustic capacity that the shape remained unchanged throughout the ages. There are, of course, many other string instruments; harpsichord, clavichord, spinet, virginal, these were large and more often than not resembled furniture. The hand instruments like the lute were the viol and violin family. There were trumpets, bassoons, oboes, keyed flutes etc, which were the wind section. Illustrations show the various types throughout the period.

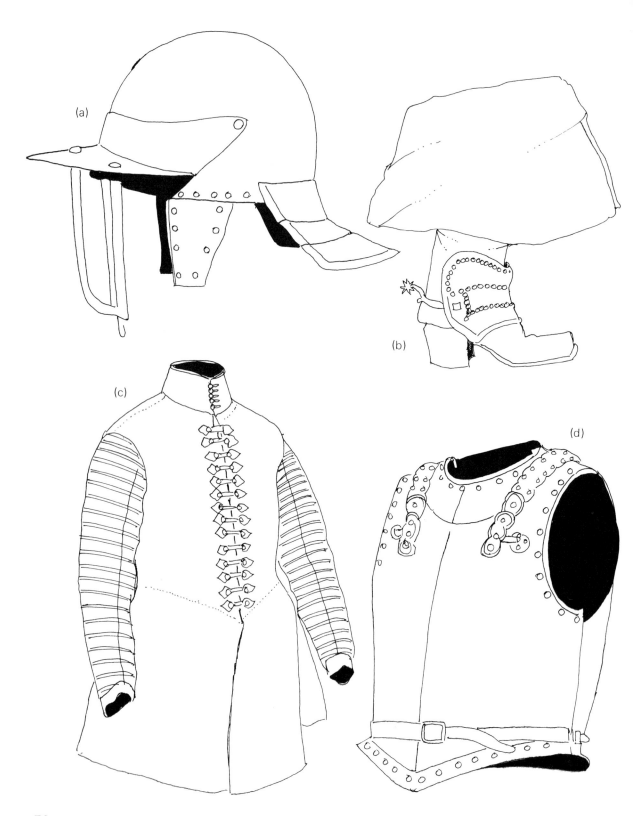

With regard to the *costume properties*, the true definition is those which are usually worn separate from the actual costume, or those items which are carried on the person or by hand. Such articles would include the steel collar or gorget 1600-1650 worn both by civilians (as affectation) or by soldiers as protection. Daggers, which were carried for self-protection, went out of fashionable wear about 1605, before this date they were popular. Small swords from *c* 1660 were worn from a shoulder belt or baldrick up to about 1700. This small sword or rapier type had a comparatively short blade of about 75 cm (29 in.) long, in comparison with the long, heavy great sword previously carried by cavalier and commonwealth soldiers alike.

This newer invention of the rapier came from France. It is important to remember, as indeed it is the property department and costume designer's job to remember, that the period was a formal one; dress and equipment were laid down by unwritten but inflexible laws, which stated that a man who had any pretension to gentility could not be seen without a small sword at his side. Therefore it becomes an indispensible costume 'prop' accessory for this period.

Costume jewellery for the period of 1600-1650 was elaborate — neck chains for men and long chains often worn slung from one shoulder to round the waist for women. Both sexes wore pendants, bracelets, lockets and pomanders. Rings were very popular, worn on fingers and thumbs; ladies frequently wore a ring on the fourth finger which was secured to the wrist by a fine chain.

Hand mirrors were carried by ladies and the elegant fops. Long walking sticks were affected and from about 1660 these were decorated with ribbon loops or tasselled cords. Combs and snuffboxes were also carried. Fans, either the large feather variety or the smaller folded (hand-painted) hand fans were considered as everyday accessories. The larger fans usually had heavily decorative handles.

The *mask* was very much a part of this period of costume. The whole 'vizard' masks covered the face and were usually oval in shape and held by a small bead which was attached to the inner surface of the mask and clenched between the teeth. The half 'Loo' mask obscured the upper half of the face and was secured by ties round the head. Masks were

Cavalry uniform, mid-seventeenth century (a) Three barred lobster pot helmet (b) Bucket topped boot (c) Knee length leather buff coat with sleeves braided with metallic strips (d) Breast and back plates

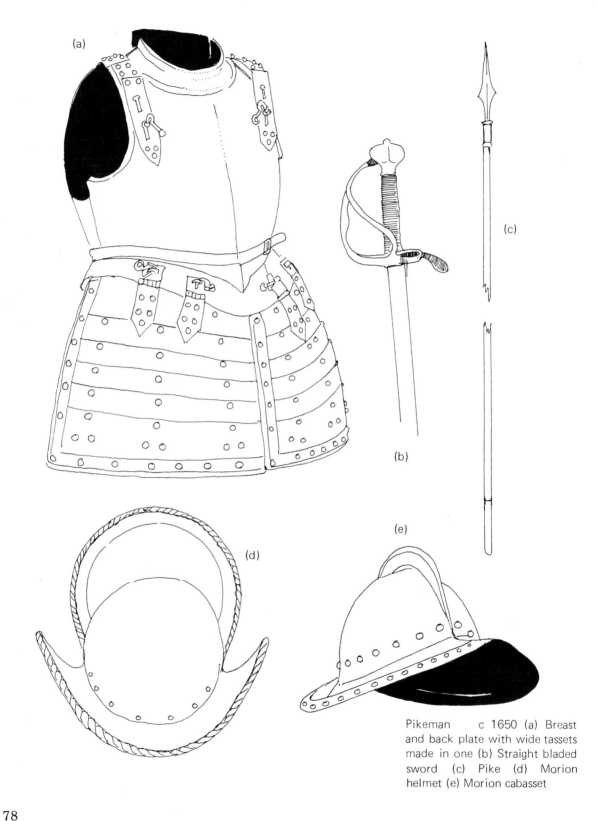

Pikeman c 1650 (a) Breast and back plate with wide tassets made in one (b) Straight bladed sword (c) Pike (d) Morion helmet (e) Morion cabasset

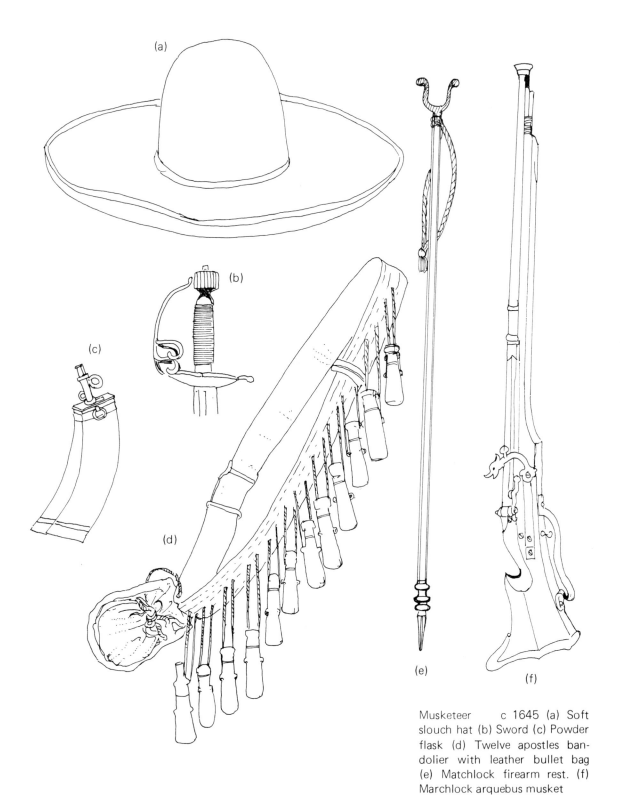

(a)

(b)

(c)

(d)

(e)

(f)

Musketeer   c 1645 (a) Soft
slouch hat (b) Sword (c) Powder
flask (d) Twelve apostles bandolier with leather bullet bag
(e) Matchlock firearm rest. (f)
Marchlock arquebus musket

79

Pistols and powder flask shapes
worn during the period

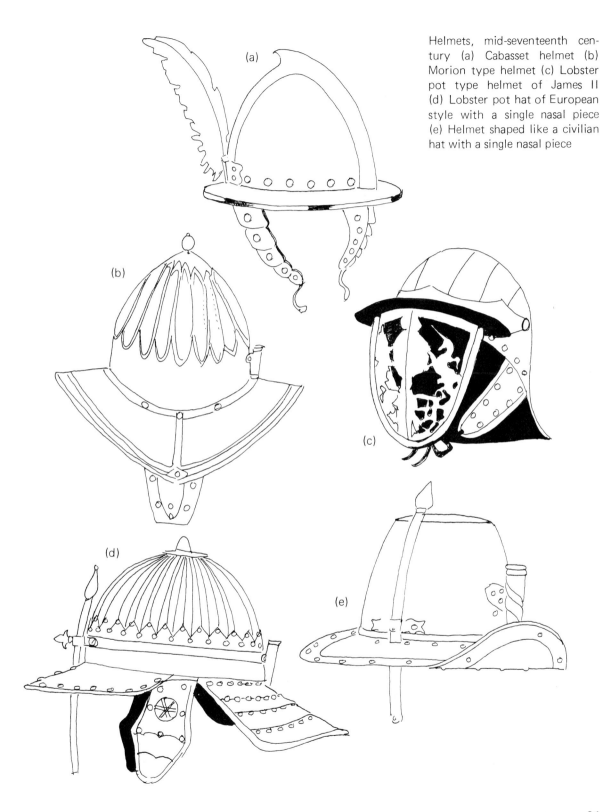

Helmets, mid-seventeenth century (a) Cabasset helmet (b) Morion type helmet (c) Lobster pot type helmet of James II (d) Lobster pot hat of European style with a single nasal piece (e) Helmet shaped like a civilian hat with a single nasal piece

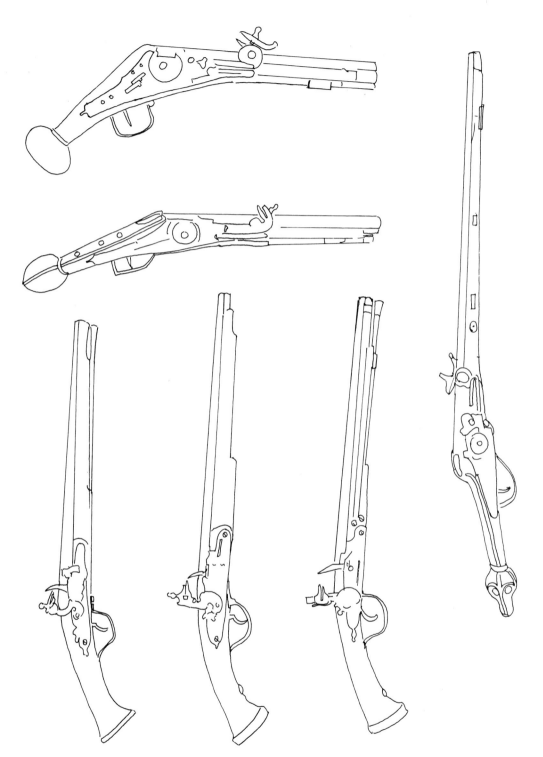

Gun shapes used during the
period as stage property reference

made from silk, taffeta, satin, velvet, highly decorated at times and were lined with animal skin or silk. The masks were worn mainly at the theatre or were used at night as complexion protectors.

Armour Now to the military field of prop-making. The custom of wearing armour lessened during the sixteenth century but was not discarded for all normal warfare until late in the seventeenth century. It was very noticeable still, both during the English Civil War of 1642-1649 and the European Thirty Years' War of 1618-1648.

The heavy armoured cuirassier (cavalry) wore breast and back plates over the buff leather knee-length coat. The most characteristic helmet in Europe of this period, and used especially during the English Civil War period was the 'lobster-tail pot' which was worn by the cuirassiers of both cavalier and Cromwell's men. These are illustrated along with the armour worn, as are those of the Pikemen soldiers. The Pikemen infantry wore similar breast-plates as the cavalry, with the exception that they had a further attachment of wide skirt-like tassets. Their helmets were either the Spanish morian type (cabasset) or were the wide brimmed pot variety, they were fitted with ear protecting flaps which were secured by ties under the chin. The musketeers wore no armour whatsoever, but carried a bandolier, with flasks, bullet bag, charges and keys or 'spanners' for the matchlock gun. They also carried their gun rests which were made of wood and stood a metre and a half high (5 ft) with a steel fork shape on the top. A coil of slow burning match was also carried.

The *weapons* were rapidly changing in function due to the widespread use of gun-powder and fire-arms. As the seventeenth century progressed pistols had shorter barrels and the wheel-lock mechanism was enclosed by a protective cage: and ornate decoration was discarded for general use. The typical military pistol had a plain wooden stock. As the musket and the pistol developed so many of the previous weapons became no more than ceremonial arms, this included mainly the halberds and partisans. Many of these became very ornamental and decorative with gilded blades and velvet covered shafts, nonetheless they made splendid 'props' for guards, who still however retained them.

A great variety of swords were still in use during the sixteenth and seventeenth centuries, many of their features were retained from earlier models (see Volume 2). For hunting purposes the wealthier classes used mainly the previous traditional weapons including the cross-bow.

During the whole of the seventeenth century the heavy matchlock gun was used by the infantry gunners. The flintlock gradually took over after this time. Many types are illustrated.

The making of these properties is very much a matter of the skill and know-how of the property department team. With the advent of modern techniques and materials almost anything is possible. Glass fibre seems to have taken over from papier-mâché, although price for price papier-mâché is still in many ways better and cheaper. Jewellery certainly has improved with the various polyester resin techniques and present a more realistic effect. Try various media and find the one which suits your purpose the best, and, as always with a production, the cheapest way.

Firearms of the seventeenth century varying from 60 cm to 1 metre (about 2 ft—1 yd)

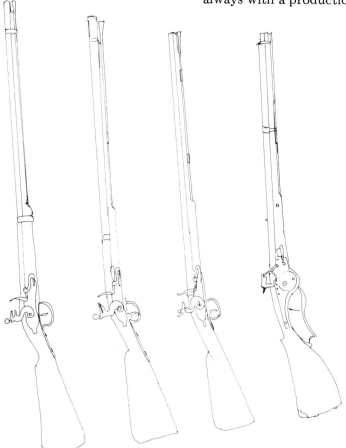

STAGE SETTINGS

We have seen that stage costume takes its shape from the body of the person who must wear it, so must the stage design fit the play, bearing in mind that the setting, like the costume, is just a part of the whole presentation. A good design should enhance the production and give the correct atmosphere, yet not overawe either the costume or the actor in its conception.

The basic architectural design of each period must be incorporated into the setting in whatever form the designer desires, realistically or symbolically. Whichever way, it must convey atmosphere and be in character.

Stage set designing is in its way quite different from all other arts. It is a wide range of creative expressions for all those who follow this type of work. It has an appeal to the imagination and carries one along from the commonplace activities of life. A good designer must possess the dramatic impulse and be able to transfer an idea to a built stage picture. Also to comprehend the aims and standards of the separate arts and have an understanding of the principles of stagecraft.

The imaginative and adventurous make the best designers, people who can project and stimulate a close link between producer, costume designer and the working staff of the production team. A good designer can link, individually and in co-operation, all of these in a combined effort. The set-designer must produce the area of the action and establish the mood and atmospheric impression, no mean feat.

So with an understanding and appreciation of all the allied arts that go into making a production, it is wise to remember that suggestion and simplicity are the key notes of a good design. Too much finicky detail in decoration often results in confusion and a bad design. Colour has a definite place in the set, its greatest function is to emphasize the mood of the play; that is, to create the true atmosphere. There are no rules to what colour may be used on the stage,

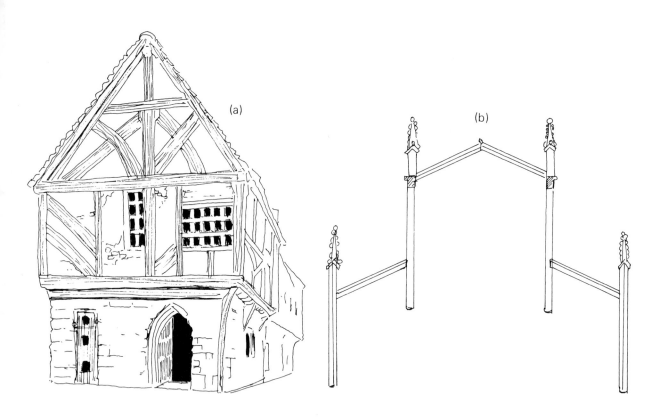

(a) Timbered houses used in all periods (b) Simple architectural shapes placed against a cyclorama background can give the correct atmosphere as door openings and windows

the science of the use of colour is learnt by practical application. It is for the set designer to decide.

There is an old Chinese proverb which says 'One picture is worth ten thousand words'. See that your design can tell in so many words, the period and atmosphere. Elizabethan plays were mostly acted in a permanent setting in the open air. Usually a wall piece with a door opening either side and a central opening with a balcony over the centre. This was often closed with a curtain, which, when open exposed a room space. The plays were more vocal than visual, the actors often describing the setting. This type of Elizabethan playhouse ceases with the Commonwealth. Modern audiences perhaps demand a little more, scenically. So knowledge of the Renaissance architectural character would be well worth a study. In this volume we cover the period of Early Renaissance during the eras of Elizabeth, 1558-1603, Jacobean 1603-1625 and the Late Renaissance of the Stuarts 1625-1689, and their European counterparts. Although both periods displayed a continuity of style, it was the variety of detail which showed the characteristic features of each period.

After the great church-building programmes of the Middle Ages, architecture became more secular in nature and with the emergence of powerful merchants, domestic mansions were built in the country. The architectural silhouette was of towers, parapets, gables and chimney stacks, set in formal gardens with lakes, fountains and pathed terraces, in a planned harmonious uniformity.

Jacobean architecture followed on similar lines, inheriting most of the Elizabethan traditions, with the exception that now Roman classical columns were incorporated in the design. Characteristic features of these periods were the Great Halls, wide staircases and the long galleries. Wide terraces with balustrades raised above garden level and broad flights of steps.

Walls were made both in brick and stone, in Jacobean times marked by a free use of the classic 'orders' one above the other. Gables of scroll-work, chimney-stacks in brick or stone work followed the Tudor style, as did the windows with their vertical mullions, leaded glass and horizontal transoms, becoming flat topped instead of arched in keeping with the level ceilings of the domestic rooms. Bay windows were also used. Arcades were incorporated in the larger dwelling houses.

(a) Arch centre piece (b) Gate set-piece, two piers at opposite ends (c) Pillar set-piece placed central or off-centre

(a)

(b)

(c)

The roofs were steep and sloping, covered in tiles, stone slabs or lead, sometimes with a mixture of all three. These roofs were trunked with gables of the Gothic style, along with low pediments of the classic period. Favourite features deriving from the Gothic style were the balustrades which were arcaded, battlemented, pierced or columned.

Roman columns of the five orders of architecture form the characteristic features of the Renaissance style. They were used in every part of the building, externally in the gables, chimney stacks and porches, and inside in doorways and the ornate fire-places. Pilasters were surrounded with 'strapwork' (plaster work which looked like entwined straps) or prismatic ornament. Mouldings were a mixture of Gothic and Roman forms. Heraldic and mythological carved figures influenced the ornamentation along with the 'strap' style and were used extensively. Interiors had carved wainscot panelling, broad stairs, wall tapestries and ornamented plaster ceilings.

The *Stuart* and *Late Renaissance architecture* incorporates the period from Charles I 1625-1649, the Commonwealth 1649-1660, Charles II 1660-1685, James II 1685-1689, William and Mary 1689-1702 and Queen Anne 1702-1714. The main influences of the Renaissance architecture came from the genius of individual architects. The forerunners of these men who dominated this development of design were

(a) Wing piece with profiled edge (b) Cut-out set-piece of garden ornament (c) Cut-out, back view

(a)

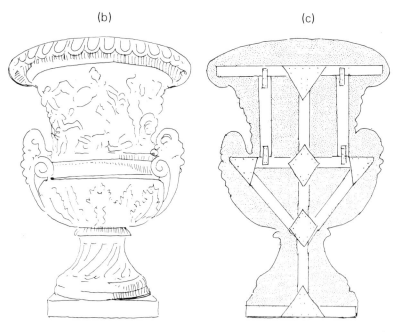

(b)

(c)

the Italian artists, Michelangelo and Palladio and in England Inigo Jones (1573-1652) and Sir Christopher Wren (1632-1723).

It is interesting to note that Inigo Jones who studied under Palladio introduced the Italian Renaissance architecture in his scenic designs for the Court Masques performed in the period 1605-1640. The Commonwealth period sadly neglected many of Inigo Jones's designs and they remained uncompleted.

Wren, the other great personality during this period, unlike Jones, came under the French Renaissance influence and studied under the great French architects Bernini and Mansart.

The late Renaissance architecture had imposing facades with exaggerated symmetry. The walls followed the previous style of stone, sometimes simulated with stucco or with red brickwork. The interior designs were panelled overall from floor to ceiling, the wall surface being divided into dado, large panels and moulded cornice.

Arcades were formed from columns of classical design. More formal were the doorways which later developed special features. The sloping roofs were now often without gables, the cornice being the main feature of the buildings.

Built rostrum shaped piece for interior or exterior decoration, all periods

Low-pitched pediments outlined the ends of the roofs in preference to the steep gables. Balustrades remained in vogue and in the general design.

The main silhouette was changing to domes, cupolas and steeples under the guidance of Sir Christopher Wren. Mouldings following the classical order columns became bolder in design and took on a more classical look. The Gothic influence was gradually lost as the Italian Renaissance tradition took over.

The Adam brothers' simple classical traditional style proved very popular.

Although stage properties are a great part of the interior architecture it is easier to treat these under a separate heading, keeping, as per theatre tradition, the scenery and the property as two distinct departments.

To the set designer comes the task of producing an area to be played in. Knowing the facts of the period he/she must develop and expand this knowledge to create the atmosphere and 'feel' that should be imparted to the audience on the raising of the curtain.

STAGE LIGHTING

The Medieval and Elizabethan theatres depended mostly on daylight for their source of illumination. With the coming of the indoor closed-in theatre the problem of lighting began, so over the centuries a new theatre art form came into being, that of stage lighting.

Lighting has developed over the years to be one of the most important facets of all the theatre arts. It has opened up a new dimension of stage design. Without the aid of scenic design a designer can, with the use of light and colour, produce almost any desired atmospheric effect.

But do not be carried too far away with light and colour, however fascinating these may seem. Lighting can be disciplined to take its place within the stage design group. Its important functions are to light the various characters in the play and to bring, via colour, the mood and atmosphere of the play. Like the costume and the set design it must not overawe the production but play its part, subordinate to the actor.

The theatre today is dependent on light. The most obvious reason is naturally visibility, so that the audience can see what is taking place. The light sources show them the parts of the stage which are needed to be seen and conversely obscures or suppresses parts which should not be seen. Such is the magic of theatre stage lighting. It reflects the mood of the play: happy, sinister, sad, warm, cold, reality or fantasy, yet such is the power of light that it conveys the sense of reality. To the actors and actresses, by its intrinsic character, light can accentuate their roles by a single effect of colour or change in depth and intensity to follow the ever-changing atmosphere of the unfolding historical drama.

So much can be achieved by stage lighting, especially if used not just for its natural main function to illuminate the characters, the costumes and the stage setting, but as an artistic medium to give light and shade in varying values.

In which case the designer should try to understand the science of light. Well designed sets and costumes can be utterly spoilt and have no impact with incorrect lighting.

Unfortunately this chapter is much too short to discuss at length the psychological and symbolic significance of colour but it is my hope that the historical costume and set designers will familiarise themselves with this very important part of theatre art.

CHOOSING A PLAY

Maxwell Anderson
Elizabeth the Queen
Mary of Scotland

Francis Beaumont and
   John Fletcher
*Knight of the Burning
   Pestle*

Beulah Maria Dix
Alison's Lad

Edward Bulwer-Lytton
Richelieu

Pedro Calderon De La Barca
Life's a Dream
The Combat of Love
Jealousy
The Lady and her Maid

Pierre Corneille
Le Menteur
Le Cid
Horace
Agésilas
Polyeucte Martyre
La Mort de Pompée
*Cinna ou la Clémence
   d'Auguste*
Rodogune
Nicomède

A play is the heart-beat of the theatre, and from it stems all the dramatic motivation which this volume has attempted to explain. It is the starting point, its ingredients are people, happenings, time and location. The play is not fiction, the plot is performed by characters and the theme revealed in the presence of an audience.

The study and analysis of a play is not so difficult a problem if one starts in a methodical manner. The play reading is to tell us what the author is trying to convey to his audience, the motive, dramatic or otherwise, basically, the plot. Next study the items of interest that combine in the build-up to the climax which must play their subordinate parts to the ultimate main action. The reading should be carried out three or four times, until all the minor situations of the plot have been placed into their respective status in order of impact and importance.

If there is a problem it is an overwhelming problem of selection, the plays of the sixteenth and seventeenth century were much more varied than the earlier period. The reign of Elizabeth I in England was one of the greatest periods of drama due to the increase of a large group of actors and writings of the period.

The greatest development in play writing took place in England and France. The brilliant works of Shakespeare, Molière and Corneille live on.

The list of plays I have compiled as a guide to the periods in this volume are a mixture of tragedy and comedy. Most of these have been dramatised over the years by theatre groups, school drama study and dramatic societies.

All of these can be simply staged and played in the costumes of the period, although later in the eighteenth century some were played in Greek or Roman classical costume. The obvious first choice for this period are the surviving plays of that swashbuckling era of the Restoration.

Don Sanche d'Aragon
Mélite
Clitandre
La Veuve
L'Illusion
La Galerie du Palais
La Suivante
Le Palais Royale
Médée
Héraclius
La Suite du Menteur
Théodore, Vierge et
    Martyre
Andromède
Pertharite
Suréna
Roi des Lombards
Oedipe
Sertorius
La Conquête de la Toison
    D'or
Othon
Attila Roi des Huns
Tite et Bérénice
Pulchérie

Thomas Corneille
Timocrate
Ariane
Le Comte d'Essex

William Congreve
The Way of the World

Clemence Dane
Will Shakespeare

James Fagan
And so to Bed

George Farquhar
The Recruiting Officer
Beaux' Stratagem

Anthony Hope
English Nell

Victor Hugo
Ruy Blas

Ben Jonson
Epicoene, or The Silent
    Woman
Volpone
Every Man in his Humour

Paul Kester
Sweet Nell of Old Drury

Edward Knoblock
My Lady's Dress

Thomas Kyd
The Spanish Tragedy

J B P De Molière
Les Précieuses Ridicules
L'Avare
L'Ecole des Maris
Les Fâcheux
Le Misanthrope
Le Médecin Malgré Lui
Tartuffe
Monsieur de Pourceaugnac
Le Bourgeois Gentilhomme
Dom Juan
Les Femmes Savantes
Le Malade Imaginaire
Dom Garcie de Navarre
L'Ecole des femmes

Amphitryon
George Dandin
Les Amants
    Magnifiques

Eugene O'Neill
The Fountain

Jean Racine
Thébaïde
Alexandre le Grand
Bajazet
Andromaque
Les Plaideurs
Bérénice
Mithridate
Phèdre

Edmond Rostand
Cyrano de Bergerac

William Shakespeare
Twelfth Night
Much Ado about Nothing
Love's Labour's Lost
The Taming of the Shrew
Two Gentlemen of Verona
Romeo and Juliet
The Merchant of Venice
Measure for Measure
All's Well that Ends Well
As You Like It

George Bernard Shaw
The Dark Lady of the
    Sonnets

William Wycherley
The Country Wife
Plain Dealer

INDEX